MADE FOR

Made for Freedom: Loving, Defending, and Living God's Gift, Copyright © 2012, Scepter Publishers, Inc. for the English Edition.

Made for Freedom: Loving, Defending, and Living God's Gift is a translation of *Libertad vivida con la furerza de la fe* (Fifth Edition) © 2010 by Ediciones Rialp, S. A., Calle Alcalá, 290, 28027.

Copyright © 2012, Scepter Publishers, Inc.
P.O. Box 211, New York, N.Y. 10018
www.scepterpublishers.org

English translation by Bernard Browne

Text and cover design by Rose Design

Printed in the United States of America

ISBN: 978-1-59417-167-3

MADE FOR
Freedom

Loving, Defending
and Living God's Gift

JUTTA BURGGRAF

 Scepter

✏ Contents

❧Prologue*

AN AFRICAN TALE

THERE IS A WELL-KNOWN AFRICAN STORY about a hunter who, while walking through the jungle, came across a recently hatched eaglet. He picked it up and carried it to his home, where he put it in his chicken coop. The king of all birds grew up with the chicks and learned to behave like one of them; he ate his corn and hopped about in the yard like the others.

One day, after many months, the man reflected on the large wings of this majestic bird and on the fact that, despite them, he had not yet learned to fly, having been cooped up his whole life. The good man repented of what he had done and decided to give the eagle his freedom. Taking him out of the coop and lifting him gently in his arms, he carried him to a nearby hill. There he pointed to the sky and said: "You are an eagle. You belong to the heavens, not to the earth. Open your wings and fly!" But the bird did not move. He looked down at the feeding chickens and hopped back to rejoin them. The man tried again: "You shouldn't demean yourself by acting like those chickens, who do nothing but quarrel with each other and constantly peck at the ground. Spread out your wings and fly!" But the young eagle became more and more confused by this demanding challenge. His whole

---

* I would like to thank my friend, Dr. Maria Salazar Sanchez, for her valuable suggestions and the generous help she gave me in correcting the Spanish text.

body trembled, and it became clear that his only desire was to return to the safety of his coop.

The hunter did not get discouraged. The next day, very early, he brought the eagle to a very high mountain. At the summit he lifted up the eagle once more and, arms extended, pointed him directly toward the brilliant morning sun, saying encouragingly: "You are an eagle. You were born to move through the air freely, to soar toward the sun. You can travel enormous distances and play with the wind. Don't be afraid. Try it! Open your wings and fly." The eagle, fascinated by the abundance of light, lifted himself in a lordly way, slowly opened his great wings, and, with a triumphant cry, began to fly—higher and higher, until he disappeared from sight.

"He who has been born with wings should use them to fly," mused the man as he descended the mountain, singing.

✍ I.

AN ORIGINAL CALL

"WE ARE ALL BORN AS ORIGINALS and die as carbon copies." So say the cynics. If we take a quick look at ourselves and our surroundings, it may seem they are not far from the truth. In our technically developed but humanly impoverished society, one finds an obvious uniformity in thinking, speaking, dressing, acting, and reacting. Passing through the great cities, we find our surroundings to be more and more artificial and the manipulation ever more aggressive. Often we have neither time nor desire to cultivate our interior selves. We allow ourselves to be easily carried along by each new fashion that arises in our culture. Ultimately, we fail to see that our life has any meaning, anything worth struggling and suffering for.

We have forgotten that we are not just *something* but *someone:* a being tenderly loved by God and called to live a unique and passionate life, a free and creative being, summoned with God's grace to overcome even the greatest obstacles we encounter on our way.

THE CHALLENGE OF FREEDOM TODAY

What is freedom? In a first attempt at defining it, we might say it is openness to the infinite. It is the radical capacity to be the protagonist of one's life. It is an immense gift that puts into play all of our potential and decisively marks our character and destiny. On the one hand, we can associate it with joy, love, and the desire for fullness, culminating in God; and on the other hand, with despair, anxiety, and absurdity. Freedom enables us to attain greatness, but it also includes the possibility of going completely off track. It involves human self-fulfillment or human self-destruction.

As humans we are confronted with certain questions: *What is the meaning of life? What are my roots? What is it that shapes my thinking and my desires?* We can look back with thanksgiving for all we have received from those who came before us, for the deeds (known or unknown) that others have accomplished. But we cannot forget that each of us has the mission to illuminate something new. Each person is unique and original. With each birth, something singularly new enters the world. The new, Hannah Arendt says, "always appears in the form of a miracle."[1] No one knows how they are going to evolve, what they will become, what they will use their talents for. The human being is not only endowed with the capacity of *proposing* an end, but also of *being* its own end: it is called to make itself. It can develop its talents and convert its life—and itself—into something truly great. One can expect the unexpected, the unheard of, from human beings.

Every person can offer many surprises to the world: new thoughts, new words, new solutions, and unique actions.

---

1. Hannah Arendt, *La condición humana* (*The Human Condition*) (Barcelona, 1993), p. 202.

Each individual is capable of living his or her own life and being the source of inspiration and support for others. At times, it is good to recapture the outlook of a child, to open ourselves to our own novelty and that of every person, and thus discover the challenge found in each situation. The world will be what we make of it—at least *our* world and our life are what we make of it.

We are free, in spite of adverse circumstances that may surround and influence us. And we not only have the right but also the *duty* of exercising our freedom, precisely in this subtly tyrannizing world in which we have been called to live. No one should turn himself or herself into an "automaton," without face or originality. It is more necessary than ever that we become conscious of the great richness of human life and seek paths to become "more" human, and not persons who are timid, afraid, and sorrowful.[2]

THE DIVINE PLAN

Contrary to the official propaganda spread in recent years, God is not the enemy of freedom: on the contrary, he is freedom's creator, its great friend and protector. Our freedom is a gift *from him.* To demonstrate this, we have to go back to our origins and look at what happened "in the beginning," when the human person was called into existence.

According to the first book of the Bible—the book of Genesis—at the culminating moment of his creative work, God pronounced the solemn words that still resound today:

---

2. In fact, it is not surprising that we encounter in our day people thirsting for an authentic life worthy of man, people who do not repress the "anxieties" of their heart and who experience a true hunger for freedom and meaning. See Vatican II, Pastoral const. *Gaudium et Spes* (GS), 4, 9, and 17.

"Let us make man in our image, after our likeness."[3] Why did he use the plural? According to a Jewish story, he would not have done that to indicate his majesty. Rather, the story continues, it is as if the Creator were already speaking with the new creature who was at the point of coming forth from his hands: "Come on, you and I together will create man. If you don't help me, I won't be able to make a finished man, a personality." This was an allusion to the freedom of the person, who "builds himself" through his own acts, being himself the one who constructs his life. If we open ourselves to his help, God will breathe into us the breath of his Spirit so that we *become who we are*, that unique person the world expects us to be and that we owe to the world.[4] According to Guardini, a successful life begins with an apparently very simple determination: "A man decides to live like a man."[5]

Who was I in God before I was born? From all eternity, the Creator had a marvelous idea of every one of us. He entrusted each of us with an original project. If we focus on that project and try to carry it out, it will not be difficult to fill our lives with meaning and to find our own path through the world.

Representing all of us, the prophet Isaiah said, "The Lord hath called me from the womb, from the bowels of my mother he hath been mindful of my name."[6] These words

---

3. Gen 1:26.

4. See Bl. John Paul II, encyclical *Veritatis Splendor* (*VS*), 39: "Not only the world, however, but also man himself has been entrusted to his own care and responsibility. God left man "in the power of his own inclination" (Sir 15:14), that he might seek his Creator and freely attain perfection. Attaining such perfection means personally building up that perfection in himself."

5. Romano Guardini, *Tugenden: Meditationen über Gestalten sittlichen Lebens* (Mainz-Paderborn, 1987, third ed.), p. 84.

6. Is 49:1 (Douay version).

express the originality of every human being. In calling man "by name," God—the eternally New—has given to each *his* vocation, *his* mission, *his* specific talent for the world's enrichment.

Those words also express the great love of God that never fails. God loves us not only in the past, not just at the moment of birth, but each day and in each instant: he loves us in life. It is precisely this eternal and ever new love that is the basis of our freedom. We are free from the moment someone loves us and accepts us with affection.

GOD'S LOVE

To give love, one must first find it in one's own life. The "street kids" of Rio de Janeiro are a clear example: many of them are drawn toward criminal behavior, lack self-respect, and don't even fear death, because they see no place for themselves in the world. They have been unable to develop that "original trust"[7] that other children experience from their parents and within their families. And since they lack this, they are filled with "original anguish": they feel rejected or controlled, coerced and condemned, and, above all, gravely wounded within.[8]

On the other hand, someone with original trust can look at his surroundings with confidence. His fundamental outlook is grounded in a profound confidence in himself and in the trustworthiness of human beings—trustworthiness

---

7. The concept of "original trust" (*Urvertrauen*) comes from Erik Erikson. See Erikson, *Identität und Lebenszyklus* (Frankfurt, 1966).

8. This interior woundedness can be the cause of our "becoming children-adults with a lack of interior freedom and sheepishness." See John Bradshaw, *Das Kind in uns* (*The Child in Us*) (Munich, 1992), p. 66.

in which there shines something of the faithfulness of God, who is always on our side.

The situation of the street children shows the urgency of helping everyone understand that God loves them passionately. Then they too can hear in the depths of their hearts those words spoken to the prophet Isaiah: "Fear not, for I have redeemed you; I have called you by name, you are mine. When you pass through the waters I will be with you; and through the rivers, they shall not overwhelm you. . . . Because you are precious in my eyes, and honored, and I love you."[9]

In the Old Testament, we see that it was not only in important events but also in everyday life that the chosen people discovered Yahweh's presence, his love and tenderness, his forgiveness and faithfulness. God showed from the beginning that he wanted to be close to men. He made himself accessible to them; he went to meet them, he saved, protected, and guided them, and he filled them with innumerable good things.[10] "Can a woman forget her sucking child, that she should have no compassion on the son of her womb? Even these may forget, yet I will not forget you. Behold, I have graven you on the palms of my hands."[11]

While Israel frequently turned away from the right path, God always showed himself to be faithful and kind.[12] He accepted the people in their weakness and forgave their guilt. "The mountains may depart and the hills be removed, but my steadfast love shall not depart from you . . . says the Lord, who has compassion on you."[13]

---

9. Is 43:1–4.
10. See Ps 36:6–8; 103:1–14; 145:1, 7–9.
11. Is 49:15–16; See Mic 7:18–19.
12. See Ex 34:6–7; Neh 9:17; Jer 31:20; Ps 103:3–4, 8–14, Is 41:9–10, 43:3–4.
13. Is 54:10; See Hos 11:9.

Man does not draw out or merit God's mercy. God's love is before man's existence, and is the one sure thing that exists. "Thy steadfast love is great to the heavens. . . . [Thy] steadfast love endures forever."[14]

In the fullness of time, God manifested himself to us as Father, Son, and Holy Spirit. The Trinity is, in a certain sense, "interior life" and divine "intimacy" itself; it is a mystery of deep communion, a mystery of mutual and constant giving. This allows us to see—although only from afar— what it means to say, "God is love."[15]

That God is himself life and love signifies his complete blessedness and is the foundation of our hope in the midst of suffering and death. The most profound reality of our world and the root of our existence is divine love, an outpouring of life and happiness.

In the New Testament God shows us with all clarity that his devotion to man has no limits.[16] He is ready to share our needs and our sufferings. For this reason, he hides his divinity and makes himself present in Jesus Christ.[17] He freely lowered himself in order to heal us on the deepest level of our being and draw us to the heart of his Trinitarian love. He invites us to live life with him.[18] He wants to share his intimacy with us and to maintain with each person an unrepeatable dialogue.

---

14. Ps 57:10; 117:2.

15. 1 Jn 4:8–16. For a Christian, not to believe in the love of God is not to believe in God, because our God "is love." See Søren Kierkegaard, *Il vangelo delle sofferenze* IV: "If God is not love, he simply does not exist." In idem, *Opere,* ed. by Cornelio Fabro (Florence, 1972), p. 859.

16. Bl. John Paul II, encyclical *Redemptoris Mater* 9: "God's salvific giving of himself and his life, in some way to all creation, but directly to man, reaches one of its high points in the mystery of the Incarnation."

17. See Phil 2:6–8.

18. See *GS*, 19: "The root reason for human dignity lies in man's call to communion with God. From the very circumstance of his origin man is already invited to converse with God. For man would not exist were he not created by God's love and constantly preserved by it."

Until we discover this immense love of God for us, we live like vagabonds in a state of alienation and rootlessness, like orphans with neither home nor father.

BORN TO RESPOND

We are the fruit of a completely new call on the part of God. To be human, to be *this* human, is one's vocation, to which one must give a response no less entirely new and original. The art of living consists in discovering my true face—that image which God saw before he created me.[19]

We have a Father who loves us deeply. Our deepest identity consists in being his child, a very beloved child of God, not because of what we do, but simply because of who we are.[20] According to a Jewish tradition, Rabbi Shlomo was asked: "What is the worst thing a man can do?" He answered with a certain sadness: "The worst thing is that a man should forget that he is the son of a King."[21] Unless we understand that we have been "received by God" and "oriented toward him," we will live disoriented in this world, and our freedom will vanish.

A Christian knows he has received a great deal from men and everything from God. He receives his life as a gift. He believes not only in God's existence but in God's love—a love eternally new, present in the origin of his existence and reaching to what is deepest in him.[22]

---

19. See 1 Cor 7:17: "Let everyone lead the life which the Lord has assigned to him."

20. Man is "the only creature on earth which God willed for itself" (*GS*, 24).

21. Martin Buber, *Die Erzählungen der Chassidim* (Zürich, 1949), p. 403.

22. See Kierkegaard, *Il vangelo delle sofferenze* IV: "Oh, who knows how many call themselves Christian and perhaps live doubting if God is really love!" in idem, *Opere*, cit., p. 859.

Accepting One's Weakness

To be a Christian is to live with one's heart in the heavens, though not in the clouds. We are meant to be very much of this world and at the same time very much of God, and we are meant to develop all the dimensions of our human-Christian personality. To reach this highly attractive goal, we must imitate those pearl-fishers in the Pacific: we must dive all the way down to the bottom in order to propel ourselves back to the air and sunlight. We must fully accept our human condition, with all its limitations and weaknesses, failures and anxieties.

We are invited to follow Christ, who descended to us here on earth, becoming man, so that we could find the courage also to descend to our own reality. Only in that way can we ascend to God.

St. Augustine said that God is closer to us than we are to ourselves.[23] He is also more loyal to us than we are. Sometimes we are not loyal to ourselves—we are neither authentic nor true. We don't want to see ourselves as we really are. In our culture we soon learn to be "strong" and to defend ourselves in the jungle of life. Vulnerability is dangerous and therefore not allowed. We must subtly conceal our dark places and fears, our needs and weaknesses. This is how some people attain a certain social recognition, but they pay a great price for it. They deny their own humanity and renounce a life of freedom.

We are a divine project with God-given limits, fragile and impotent in so many ways. Perhaps it's a matter of intellectual limitations or limitations in mental stability, of burdens received from our parents or other relatives that determine our family, social, or professional situation.

---

23. See St. Augustine, *Confessions* III, 6.

Perhaps without admitting it to anyone, even themselves, many people feel insecure in the depths of their hearts. Despising themselves and wishing to hide it, they may present themselves as excessively tough or surround themselves with an air of importance. Consider the man who can't wait quietly for a friend in front of a restaurant; he immediately reaches for his cell phone or some other electronic device in order to keep himself preoccupied.

One way of hiding an inferiority complex is to call attention to oneself. Feelings of inferiority can be hidden behind arrogant behavior. Such a person may construct a façade of self-assurance and contempt for others. Behind the façade, however, there is no beautiful building, just a poor shanty in which he or she wants to hide. For other people, hiding takes the form of ostentation about money or titles. Yet what matters is not an outward show of self-assurance but the inner experience of deep, underlying worth by which we know ourselves to be truly strong.

We can also observe the opposite phenomenon. Some people who are unsure of themselves behave childishly: they constantly need the approval of others, they seek a good reputation at all costs, they are only at peace if others smile and indulge them.

Often our self-image comes from the opinions others have of us, from the positions we occupy and the roles we play, from our work and social position, from our health or our sickness. We define ourselves by success, by results, by the relationships we develop. But in this way we make ourselves blind to our true reality; we become more and more dependent on others and slaves of our own "image."

An old proverb says, "Success is not a divine name." To reach happiness, we need to have the heart of a child. Is it possible to grow into a new freedom if we are not conscious of this lack of freedom? Can we desire to see if we are not aware that we are blind? God himself invites each of us to follow this descending path, just as he did; he calls all of us to simplicity. I am not an artificial structure, fragile and constantly at risk. I am what I am in God's eyes: a poor child, possessing nothing, receiving everything, infinitely loved and protected. Whoever does not go out of his self-sufficiency and accept his poverty, "whoever does not receive the kingdom of God like a child," can be sure that he "shall not enter it."[24] Intimacy with God follows the way of childhood, interior poverty, and detachment.[25] This is the way that frees us from so many superfluous attachments and enables us to say yes to what we are and to our circumstances.

The first condition for having a positive influence on the world is a wholehearted acceptance of ourselves as we are. We are strongest when we are most ourselves, when we accept our reality.

Trusting in God's Strength

Many people with insufficient self-esteem are counseled to focus on their strong points. This can be good advice. But if behind it is the idea that only the strong are valuable, the advice won't help us much. "For a very long time I considered low self-esteem to be some kind of virtue. I had been warned so often against pride and conceit that I came to consider it a good thing to deprecate myself. But now I realize that the real sin is to deny God's first love for me, to ignore my original goodness. Because without

---

24. Mk 10:15; Mt 18:1–4.
25. See Ps 8:3.

claiming that first love and that original goodness for myself, I lose touch with my true self and embark [on a destructive path]."[26]

Truly believing in our divine dignity gives us a sane appreciation of our own worth. My deepest core is something that comes directly from God; it is a mystery. It is God's original image of me. Convincing oneself of one's own value is not so difficult for someone who knows himself or herself to be unconditionally loved and supported by God. "Don't undervalue yourself, because God doesn't undervalue you," says a proverb of the East.

Too often our lives lack passion. We steer clear of the obscure depths of life in order to avoid pain. Thus we do not reach the heights either. We live in bourgeois mediocrity, avoiding every "excess." The man who hides behind a thick wall, closed off to transcendence, neither is in contact with himself nor can he open himself to the world. To do that, one must "disarm" oneself, accept one's vulnerability, recognize one's hang-ups, faults, and deficiencies, and finally renounce human security. God's help will not be lacking. God wants to show his strength precisely in the weakness of man;[27] therefore, he usually chooses what is weak and insignificant in the eyes of the world.[28]

Jesus touches on this mystery in the parable of the nuptial banquet that a king arranges for his son. Those who enjoy a good reputation in society, people undoubtedly virtuous and religious, reject his invitation. They have other things to do; they are too busy. On the other hand, the poor, the crippled, and the lame are available; they come and fill

---

26. Henri Nouwen, *The Return of the Prodigal Son: A Story of Homecoming* (New York: Doubleday, 1992), p. 107.
27. See 2 Cor 12:9.
28. See 1 Cor 1:27.

the hall.[29] The order of things has been inverted: the little ones come closer to God; the outsiders are the chosen ones.

God can do splendid things with my miseries. This is why I can say yes to the most defective and frustrating realities I discover in the depths of my heart. As St. Thérèse of Lisieux says, "Love is so powerful that it knows how to take advantage of everything, of the good and the bad that there is in me."[30] Having a healthy sense of one's worth implies recognition of one's lights as well as one's shadows, heights, and depths, the divine and the human. Someone who can confess his own faults before others is truly strong. Pope Benedict XVI, when he was still a cardinal, told an interviewer that he suffered as a student because he was the last in sports while he'd always been first in everything else.[31] A person is also strong if he can remain calm when others censure him for acting in accord with his conscience. To be oneself means to feel free and clean. Not to be oneself means to feel alienated and stained.

In the end, we see that we have many more possibilities than we thought—to say nothing of the marvels God can work in us if we are united to him.

Becoming "Yourself"

Jesus knows that we are tempted always to want to be like the "kings of the nations"[32]—to be seduced by what is great, by power and riches, pleasures and privileges. But if we seek these things compulsively, we not only separate

---

29. See Mt 22:1–14; Lk 14:15–24.

30. Thérèse of Lisieux, *Manuscrito Autobiografico* A, 53, in *Obras completas* (Burgos, 3rd ed. 1998).

31. See Joseph Ratzinger (Benedict XVI), Interview with Martin Lohmann, Bayrischer Rundfunk (Bavarian Broadcasting), December 28, 1998, 8:15 pm.

32. Lk 22:25.

ourselves from God—creating new gods—but we alienate ourselves from ourselves, deforming our nature and rejecting the condition of being those whom God has loved from eternity. In this way we place ourselves voluntarily in what has been called "self-created immaturity."[33]

From the beginning of our life, we find ourselves before an undefined horizon. Someday we must ask ourselves: "What will I do with my life? In the face of the multiple possibilities before me, I have the *task* of being myself." This was well expressed in a work by the writer Calderon de la Barca, *El gran teatro del mundo* (The Great Theater of the World). Its central idea has inspired many similar dramas in other parts of the world.

In one version, the principal characters are a prince, a doctor, and a beggar. The prince is a tyrant who makes his subjects suffer. At the end of his life, he is condemned by God. The poor beggar also is condemned because he is filled with resentment and hatred, had committed injustices, and made his wife and children suffer. But the doctor is saved. He is an honorable man and, more than that, a competent professional who did good to others.

The message of this work isn't merely social criticism. Clearly it is not good that people are poor, and all of us are called to work for a just distribution of the goods of the earth. But this literary work is saying something else: What really matters is that each one gives his best, that he develops the talents he has received for the benefit of others and in this way becomes what God envisaged for him.

It's a mistake to compare oneself with others, since that can lead to both pride and envy. God wants different things

33. Immanuel Kant, *"Respuesta a la pregunta: Que es la Ilustracion?"* in *Que es la Ilustración?* (Madrid, 1988), p. 9.

from me than he wants from you. Roses should not dream of being orchids. "The person God loves with the tenderness of a Father, the person he wants to touch and transform with his love, is not the person we'd have liked to be or ought to be. It's the person we are. God doesn't love 'ideal persons' or 'virtual beings.' He loves actual, real people."[34]

We're all different. And being different, each person can reflect some particular aspects of the goodness and beauty of the Savior differently from those that others express.[35] Each one can present Christ in a new and original way, as he has never before been manifested, as no one will ever manifest him again. Here is life's most profound meaning. To realize it, each of us must really become himself or herself. We must accept ourselves as we are and be accepted in this way by others—with our own talents, limitations, and life situations. Reality is not a rock one sits on resignedly, but a trampoline on which one must step firmly in order to jump to a better reality. Each person should become happy and make others happy, but only through fidelity to oneself, which is fidelity to the divine plan for one's life. Freedom is given to us *for others*. It is our instrument for living with others, contributing to human development—being faithful to oneself and making oneself better in order to serve others better. Love for freedom, at its core, is nothing other than love *for others*.[36]

A story is told about a wise rabbi who was admired and loved throughout the whole country. People said this very happy man had a son who was his equal. A young man who came to the village and knew the rabbi was curious to meet the son of such a great person, so he went to the village some

---

34. Jacques Philippe, *Interior Freedom* (New York: Scepter Publishers, 2007), p. 32.
35. See Rom 12:6.
36. See 1 Pet 4:10: "As each has received a gift, employ it for one another, as good stewards of God's varied grace."

distance away where the rabbi's son lived. The rabbi's son invited him to his home, and after spending several days with him, the young man exclaimed: "How can they say you're the same as your father? You are completely different. Certainly you too are a great personality, but you have a different way of thinking and feeling, a different way of solving problems, other tastes and interests. . . . " "Of course," the rabbi's son replied, smiling, "but despite that, we're the same. My father is an original, and I'm an original."

A person is happy when he fulfills his own personal truth. He "constructs" himself through his free actions; he is the artist of his own existence: he makes not only things but himself. Our life is not something given, determined once and for all. It is something to be accomplished, a project we must carry out. To be free means "to be open to possibilities that we convert into projects."[37] The art of living lies in developing the talents we have received. It comes down to this: "Follow your path, know yourself, realize yourself! Know what kind of person you can become! Discover your original, individual, inimitable mold, which God has created for you alone. And arm yourself with courage to live according to this mold."

Then begins one's personal and unique history. The man who uses his freedom begins to live his own life. He introduces something new into the world. Not by what he *does*, but by what he *is*. He wants to be that which God has wanted from all eternity.

The freedom we enjoy constitutes the greatest gift we have received upon coming into this world; it can be strengthened and elevated by grace. We should have a clear awareness of how valuable it is, and we should struggle to maintain it, defend it, and grow continually in it.

---

37. Alejandro Llano, *El futuro de la libertad* (Pamplona, 1985), p. 9.

~2.

INTERIOR FREEDOM

FREEDOM IS A PERSONAL AND INTIMATE experience of man. It is rooted very deeply in our nature. It is not enough simply to say that it's a characteristic of voluntary acts, as has traditionally been said. Freedom is something more original and elemental; it reaches to the depths of the person. It is not merely a property of one's acts, but a constitutive element of one's *being*. It signifies at the same time a radical "being with oneself" and a great opening to reality.

We've seen that we are called to be protagonists of our lives, to seek our own path, not letting ourselves be drawn by inertia toward what is softest and easiest but faithfully following the interior life—with a degree of independence from the world around us—in order to succeed in becoming what God had in mind when he spoke our name. Certainly, it is not always possible to realize externally everything we want, but the true adventures are the interior ones that no one can prevent.

THE INTIMATE SPACE OF THE PERSON

As he grows, a man gradually discovers that he has an interior space that in some way is at his disposition. Essentially, he begins to see that it doesn't depend on his parents or his teachers, on the media or public opinion. He discovers a space where he is alone with himself; he is free. He discovers his intimacy. More than possessing a certain "interiority," which animals also have, a person enjoys a certain dominion over his or her interior world and can communicate it externally or not, depending on whether or not it contributes to his or her fulfillment and that of others.[1]

"Thoughts are free," says an old German popular song. It is easy to see why singing it was forbidden in the Third Reich. But this command not to sing it, so typical of a totalitarian regime, only led to it being sung with more enthusiasm in private settings or in people's hearts, where commands cannot reach and intruders can't enter.

Intimacy refers to the interior world—that world within me, of which I have some consciousness; it is the sanctuary of the human. The intimate is what only the individual knows, that which is most one's own. I can enter within myself, and there no one can seize me. In some way, *I possess myself at the source*; *I am master of myself.* This possession of self is characteristic of the spirit.

When I am "within" myself, I readily see how unnecessary and even ridiculous it is to seek the affirmation and applause of others. A person's value does not depend on oth-

---

1. In speaking of intimacy, we are referring to "that deep and creative center which is not susceptible to further analysis, beyond which consciousness does not reach, and with which there are related, like the periphery of a circle to its center, conscious phenomena, or all that is objectively perceived, imagined and thought." James F. T. Bugenthal, *La estructura de la personalidad* (*The Structure of Personality*) (Barcelona, 1968), p. 515f.

ers; it does not depend on praise or gestures of affirmation that one may or may not receive. We are more than what we appear to be on the outside. There is a space within us to which others do not have access. It is our interior homeland, a space of silence and calm. "Unless we discover that most ancient truth," says a contemporary psychologist, "we will be condemned to wander about seeking consolations where they don't exist—in the outside world."[2]

LIVING IN ONE'S OWN HOME

A man is free in his own home. Unfortunately, many people are not "with themselves"—they are always with others. They don't know how to relax in their own company and think their own thoughts, because they are powerfully influenced by a pattern of behavior that is widespread in our consumer society.

Life has become continuous activity. Many people suffer from stress or chronic fatigue. Professional demands create excessive obligations, and even the demands of the entertainment industry have become burdensome. All people want to do in the evening is rest, find distraction from everyday problems, and avoid effort. The result is a certain "spiritual alienation," visible in the superficiality of one who lives only for the here and now. In our jaded consumer society, we find it difficult to stop and take a deeper look at our surroundings and ourselves.

In our world of distractions, the obstacles to self-encounter are numerous. Consider the media. Someone with

---

2. Bugenthal, *Stufen therapeutischer Entwicklung* (*Stages of Therapeutic Development*), in J. Bugenthal and Frances Vaughan (eds), *Psychologie in der Wende* (Munich, 1985), p. 217.

a compulsion to know immediately all the news from everywhere, who fears missing any big televised event, who watches one movie after another, is on his way to becoming a person unable to think on his own. No one really has time or strength to absorb all the incoming information that assails a person while simply walking down a city street.

An anecdote about the writer Ida Friederike Görres contains food for thought. Sometime back in the 1950s she was asked how she came up with such original ideas and could judge society's situation so clearly. Her answer: "I don't read any newspapers. In that way I can concentrate my powers. I find out what is important anyway in all sorts of ways." While this may not be worth imitating, it does make you stop and think. Now, several decades later, the volume of information we receive each day has multiplied enormously, while at the same time becoming more special-ized. It would be difficult for someone "to live with himself" without some distancing from the media of communication. As the Russian novelist Dostoyevsky said, "Being alone once in a while is more necessary for a normal person than eating and drinking."

But the problem we are considering is even more complex. Not only are many people *unable* to be alone with themselves, but others do not *want* to repose in themselves. They flee their own interiority. Silence frightens them; they don't *want* to be "their own friends." To avoid serious contact with their most intimate self, they take round-the-world trips, plug an iPod in their ears, or commit themselves to a thousand political, cultural, social, and even religious activities. Thus, more or less consciously, they shield themselves with a cloak of shards and shreds against intimacy with themselves.

But one who doesn't enjoy being with oneself will not enjoy being any place. A man who never comes face-to-face with himself can't have a true encounter with anyone else. Unless I am my own friend, I can't have an authentic friendship with anyone else. Unless I'm in harmony with myself, I can't sow peace around me.

Why this fleeing from interior space, which protects us against external attacks and offers us the possibility of living serenely in the midst of any kind of chaos? Isn't it curious that many reject this marvelous possibility, which lies within easy reach, to overcome life's difficulties? We begin to see the answer in considering what it means to be one's own friend.

Friendship requires profound sincerity. It can't be built on a lie. To make friends with myself therefore, I must behave with interior rectitude. This means not repressing the great questions that more or less often arise within me: "Who am I? Where did I come from and where am I going? Why was I born? Why am I on earth? What will become of all I've worked so hard for?" I cannot dodge these questions that touch the very fiber of my being.

"To possess oneself at the source" has a shadow side. I have the task of being myself, but this can be very difficult. Some therefore say, with the existentialist philosopher Jean-Paul Sartre, that man is "condemned" to be free. Others feel anxious in the face of freedom: I can make of my life what I want, but I don't know what I want. Who can help me? In my interior, I am alone with myself: Who will accompany me? Freedom is indeed a risk—the risk of failure. I can fail badly at being myself. Freedom can mean conquest, gain, progress—or the loss of all opportunities.

When I am with myself, I may experience my loneliness, disorientation, and limits. "We are alone" is the *leitmotif* proposed today by most of the writing popular with young people. Its classic expression is Hermann Hesse's

Steppenwolf: I am a poor recluse in the middle of a hostile world, without family or home, an enemy of everyone.[3]

This feeling of frustration does not permit me to be carried along by circumstances and simply *live:* day by day, newscast by newscast, week by week. Should I not make some fundamental plans and adjust my way of living to what I hear in the depths of my heart?

CHOOSING GOD

In seeking happiness, one quickly learns that complete fulfillment is not attainable. Yes, there are moments when one feels very satisfied: when you are with a loved one, when a job turns out well, in sacrificing for others, in sports and games, art and science. But these moments pass; they are like promises never entirely fulfilled. Happiness may disappear when we least expect it. Bitter disillusionments can occur. There can be frustration even in attaining a goal when we realize that our achievements are but a shadow of what we sought. Nothing in this world can be everything for man—everything we experience is finite and limited, imperfect and passing. What are we to think then? What meaning does life have? What is true human happiness?

Human beings experience the finite but hope for the infinite. Though conscious of life's brevity, we do not cease working, struggling, and searching for happiness. Our effort is aimed at the future; it points toward something we can fully realize, something total, something more than the passing experience of earthly happiness. Thus we reach out beyond anything we can experience and obtain; we are

---

3. See Hermann Hesse, *Steppenwolf: A Novel* (originally published Berlin: S. Fischer Verlag A.G., 1927).

constantly en route, never fully satisfied, forever hungering and thirsting for more truth, more justice, and more happiness. By ourselves we cannot satisfy our insatiable desire for ultimate fullness, perfect justice, and infallible truth. We waste our time in trying.

Moreover, we discover in our interior something unconditional and absolute, traditionally called the voice of conscience, which is heard in the depths of the heart advising, approving, and reproaching. To be sure, many ways of living are historically conditioned. But the radical orientation to do good and avoid evil has an absolute character. We would have to renounce our very selves to refrain from protesting injustices that cry to heaven, such as the murder of a peaceful person, and we are certain that the criminal should not triumph over his innocent victim. Nowhere in the world do we find perfect justice nor can we count on its ever being realized, yet we are unable to give up struggling for it.

The unconditional and absolute are also visible in love. In a beloved person everything can suddenly become new. In an instant, it can seem as if the course of history had been suspended: from the very center of time, we touch eternity. But human love can also be deceptive, since in it one experiences the limits and relativity of union. Longing for the infinite and eternal, we cannot attain them in this life. Sooner or later we reach a point at which our desire for union cannot be satisfied.

So we live with the tension between our finitude and imperfection and the desire for the infinite, absolute, and perfect. While experiencing the most radical solitude, one yearns for complete understanding and acceptance. "All human life is a cry directed to a Thou," observed Cardinal Ratzinger. Our situation is paradoxical. We tend toward an ultimate perfection that we cannot give ourselves. "Man infinitely transcends man," said Pascal.[4]

This tension causes anxiety, the disquiet and dissatisfaction that continually assail us. What use is living well if it doesn't bring eternal life? Is this an absurd desire? Should we shrug and forget it? In this case, life would be meaningless. But if man is not an absurd being, there must be an absolute reality corresponding to our hope for it. Our questioning and searching must be responses to the call of God heard in human conscience. Without God, the quest for absolute meaning is useless.

Only God is capable of satisfying our longings for happiness. "The desire for God is written in the human heart, because man is created by God and for God; and God never ceases to draw man to himself. Only in God will he find the truth and happiness he never stops searching for."[5]

By the fact of being an image of the infinite God, man holds in his heart an irrepressible need for the absolute and infinite. Coercion of any sort is therefore unbearable to him.[6] Man was not created to lead a narrow, sad life, but to live at peace. Only God can fulfill him: "Our heart is restless until it rests in you."[7] One who believes in God can acknowledge human greatness without denying human need; a believer can be completely realistic.

The option for God means an option for man. Only if God exists does human life have meaning. Only then is man not at sea in a cosmos deaf to his questions and needs; only then is the world not perceived as ruled by abstract laws or

---

4. Blaise Pascal, *Pensées* (New York: E.P. Dutton, 1958), p. 103.
5. *Catechism of the Catholic Church* (CCC), 27.
6. See *GS*, 17.
7. St. Augustine, *Confessions* 1,1.

blind chance or impersonal fate. Faith in God gives security. It permits—even demands—that we accept ourselves and all mankind unconditionally inasmuch as we are accepted unconditionally. All created things are marked by divine goodness. God has called them into being, loves them, and will continue loving them forever. The French philosopher Gabriel Marcel said: "To be in the world means *to be loved by God.*" A believing person has a fundamental trust in reality, which helps him live, love, and work.[8] Only in the mystery of God does the mystery of the human find its answer, an answer that does not solve the mystery but accepts it and enters deeply into it. "Only one who knows God also knows man," says Romano Guardini.

LETTING GOD ENTER OUR LIFE

God himself, the font of all life, wants to live in us more and more deeply.[9] From our deepest core, he wants to give us "life in abundance."[10] In some way or other, each of us is called to live the drama experienced by St. Augustine: "You were inside of me and I was outside. And I went outside seeking you."[11]

God asks of us a minimum of openness, availability, and acceptance of his grace: "O that today you would hearken to his voice! Harden not your hearts."[12] To encounter

---

8. "The Church holds that the recognition of God is in no way hostile to man's dignity, since this dignity is rooted and perfected in God. . . . By contrast, when a divine instruction and the hope of life eternal are wanting, man's dignity is most grievously lacerated, as current events often attest; riddles of life and death, of guilt and of grief go unsolved with the frequent result that men succumb to despair" (Vatican Council II, *Gaudium et Spes*, no. 21).

9. See Bl. John Paul II, encyclical *Dominum et Vivificantem*, 34.

10. See Jn 10:10.

11. St. Augustine, *Confessions*, 10.

12. Ps 95[94]:7–8.

God within ourselves, we have to—mysteriously—open the doors of our house.[13] In this intimate space of silence and calm within me, where no one else can enter, I do not want to be alone. I invite God to enter and be with me—and guide my life. My self-determination then consists in doing whatever he tells me.

There is no need for a multitude of external actions, which might even overwhelm us or become obsessive. Some people devote their lives to "fulfilling" their obligations and fighting tenaciously to clear away their defects until they realize that if they just ignite the fire of love in their hearts, everything becomes easy, for the fire will simply burn away those defects. The question isn't "What can I do for God?" but "How can I let myself be loved by him?" We needn't do everything by ourselves; we can be weak.[14] Man does not please God so much by his merits and virtues as by the limitless trust that he places in him. It is not necessary to capture the good will of the One who loved us first and who has the fervent desire to remain with us forever, loving us.[15]

When God lives in me, I enjoy "being with myself" and "entering my own home." There I experience a protected space in which I can be entirely myself. I shall never be alone but always accompanied by the One who loves me the most. It is not necessary to speak my own noisy thoughts to

---

13. See Bl. John Paul II: "Do not fear! Open wide the doors to Christ . . . Do not fear! Christ knows what lives inside every man. Only he knows it!" cited in Jose Orlandis, *La Iglesia catolica en la segunda mitad del siglo XX*, Madrid 1998, p. 159.

14. See 2 Cor 12:10.

15. 1 Jn 4:10. Song 3:17. See Kierkegaard, *Diario (Diary)* X 3 A 421: "God did not love us *first* once in the beginning, and then stop. He is at every moment the one who loves *first*. If anyone gets up in the morning and immediately raises his spirit toward the Lord, he has already preceded him and loved him first."

myself, or to solve by myself the small and large problems of every day. Christian life is a life of dialogue.[16]

A Christian lives mysteriously in Christ and Christ lives in him. He does not cease to be himself, but he is deeply marked by the *miracle of love:* "At the same time he is younger and older than ordinary . . . he is strong, and at the same time, weak; there is in him a harmony which influences his whole life."[17] Typically, one sees him smiling, conversation with him is pleasant, he is marked by great serenity and happiness. "Enthusiasm" in its Greek root means "divinized," God within us. When I am "with myself," then I am "alive." "The more we let God enter our life, the more we are and the more we feel that we are ourselves,"[18] and the more spontaneous and active we are. God is not something added to our actions; he is in the very core of our freedom. "Behold, the kingdom of God is in the midst of you [or 'within' you]."[19]

God calls us to a way of life that is completely new: He invites us to enter into his kingdom, not only after death, but here and now. For one who has experienced it, union with Christ becomes more important than anything else.[20] "Fullness of life" does not refer to having many experiences or giving everything a try. One can

---

16. "The dignity of man rests above all on the fact that he is called to communion with God. This invitation to converse with God is addressed to man as soon as he comes into being. For if man exists, it is because God has created him through love, and through love continues to hold him in existence. He cannot live fully according to truth unless he freely acknowledges that love and entrusts himself to his Creator." *GS* 19. See CCC, 27.

17. Jose Luis Martín Descalzo, *Razones por la alegria*, 8th ed. (Madrid, 1988), p. 45. Bl. John Paul II, *Greeting to those recently married*, Rome, January 17, 1979.

18. J. Morales Marín, "*Virgo veneranda*," in *Scripta de Maria* VIII (1985), p. 432.

19. Lk 17:20.

20. See Gal 2:19–20; Rom 6:3–10.

attend a thousand professional conferences and still have an infantile character. In contrast, someone may never have left his village and still have become a wise man. The issue isn't *doing* more but *being* more. What counts is the quality of our experiences: being really present, disposed to learn and to grow, being filled with wonder when the first crocuses come out in the spring or when one sees the color of the leaves in the fall, turning one's face to the wind, knowing how to enjoy a song, a poem, or a friend's presence.

BUILDING THE FOUNDATION ON GOD

We are called to happiness. We can attain this goal to a certain extent even in this world if we are ready to change the basis of our life and place it humbly in Christ. This means a real interior revolution: we do not rely on our own strength but exclusively on the omnipotence of God. Then the root of our action will be strong, and our life will be unified. Bl. John Paul II gave us a shining example of this. In his last years, a journalist interviewed a Vatican cardinal: "What do you think of the Pope?" he asked. "He is a very dangerous man," answered the cardinal. "Why is he dangerous?" "Because he trusts entirely in God," said the cardinal, pointing to what was probably one of the deepest and most characteristic attitudes of the Pontiff.

Bl. John Paul II was a man very much of the world and very much of God. He not only wanted to "follow" Jesus Christ but, through prayer and the sacraments, to let him enter deeply into his heart; he allowed Christ to live in him and act from within him. This explains the great attraction of a man who was like a magnet, not only for the millions of young people who flocked to his gatherings but for people of all ages and walks of life. One could feel the goodness of Christ in his presence.

God invites all of us to go along the road of trust, to risk our lives and place them in his hands. At times, we must overcome timidity and shake off the fear of risk, following a conviction that Scripture formulates like this: "He who is in you is greater than he who is in the world."[21]

Consider a tree that grows and develops from an insignificant mustard seed.[22] The tree puts down deep roots and grows very tall. People passing by can rest beside it and find relief in its shade. Here is an image of a person who is not easily overthrown. He speaks and acts from the security of faithfulness to himself and to God. Being firmly rooted in Christ, he can give protection and encouragement to others: "With the Lord on my side I do not fear. What can man do to me?"[23]

"I understood that one has to be a scandal for this world," said the philosopher Dietrich von Hildebrand. "I must joyfully accept being taken for crazy, ridiculous, and mentally retarded."[24] Although such a person might be labeled a "rebel," often he is healthier than someone considered "normal" for his conformity to social norms. But the so-called rebel has not given up his capacity for thinking for himself or his spontaneity. He says openly, without flattery, what he thinks, and he struggles, with the strength of grace, against all that demeans a man, turning him into a faceless cipher, a mere thing. He struggles against anything that makes it difficult for him to live peacefully with others, as do

---

21. 1 Jn 4:4.
22. See Mt 13:31f.
23. Ps 118:6.
24. Dietrich von Hildebrand, *Nuestra transformación en Cristo* (*Transformation in Christ*) (Madrid, 1996), p. 174.

lies, pride, prejudice, and manipulation.[25] Nothing is more revolutionary than a person who lets himself be led by the Holy Spirit. Jesus Christ predicted that through his power his disciples would expel demons, "speak in new tongues; they will pick up serpents, and if they drink any deadly thing, it will not hurt them."[26] Bl. John Paul II commented that the Christian future of a country "depends on how many people are mature enough to be nonconformists."[27]

The great saints were absolutely unconcerned with what others thought of them; they enjoyed "the glorious liberty of the children of God."[28] The experience of divine love brought them peace and courage, caused them to feel accompanied in all the crossroads of the world and also in solitude—a solitude filled with God. Incidents in the lives of Teresa of Jesus, Thomas More, and Joan of Arc, for example, recall what the New Testament says about the friends of God: "Through faith [they] enforced justice, received promises, stopped the mouths of lions, quenched raging fire, escaped the edge of the sword, won strength out of weakness, became mighty in war."[29] This was not a product of their own strength. In them was a mystery that surpassed them. We too are called courageously to resist everything that demeans the human person, making him a nonentity in the crowd, a mere thing, belittling his dignity and crushing his rights. Although the victory may not be visible in this world, it is a certainty for those united to Christ. Who can triumph over one whose victory presupposes the cross?

---

25. 1 Cor 7:23: "Do not become slaves of men."
26. Mk 16:17.
27. Bl. John Paul II cited in J. Ross, *Der Papst Johannes Paul II: Drama und Geheimnis* (Berlin, 2001, 3rd ed.), p. 93.
28. Rom 8:21.
29. Heb 11:33–34.

It was in this sense that Alfred Delp, who died in a Nazi concentration camp, said: "Man, surrender yourself to God and you will once more possess yourself. Now it is others who hold you, who torture you, who frighten you, who drag you from one hardship to another. This is the freedom that sings: there is no death that can kill us. This is the life that flows gently into a meadow that has no end."[30]

Faith for a Christian is the secret motor that drives a way of life lived in healthy independence of this passing world. Eternal life is the pole that attracts his thoughts, like a compass pointing the way to sailors, the reality that lifts their hearts just as the full moon raises the waters of the sea to high tide. Looking to Christ gives a Christian the secure confidence that no one has power over him, even though they may cause him harm. "The bended knee and the empty hands stretched forward are the free man's two original gestures."[31]

OPENING ONESELF TO OTHERS

Knowing his or her interior world and enjoying it is a consolation for anyone, and is especially attractive in adolescence, when one does not yet know one's own possibilities. But interior freedom is not a cloak behind which one isolates oneself by turning one's back on others. Someone who behaves like this easily can become an introvert, using his freedom only for himself, seeking his own independence before all else in pursuit of inviolability and separation from others, and thus he remains alone

---

30. Alfred Delp, "*Meditación del dia de Epifania de 1945,*" in idem, *Gesammelte Schriften* IV (Frankfurt, 1984), p. 219.
31. Ibid., p. 218.

and friendless. Having discovered one's own interiority, it is necessary to go to the next level: to open oneself, to manifest and exercise freedom.

We can indeed know ourselves and possess ourselves, but we also are made for communion with others. This orientation to others is part of our makeup. To be human means "to coexist, *an open intimacy.*"[32] And to be a saint consists not in being separate from others but in being united to Jesus Christ. Yes, everyone can and should fulfill himself, using the talents he has received. But this happens only by loving, by giving to others, and by going out of oneself.

Someone whose life is founded upon God cannot help but be aware of the immense tragedy of many of our contemporaries who pass through life alienated from themselves, chasing illusions. May they too discover their great dignity, enjoy being with themselves, and know themselves as beings who God has loved forever. Our deepest self-fulfillment consists in helping others be themselves and find their own path.

---

32. See Leonardo Polo, *El descubrimiento de Dios desde el hombre* (*The Discovery of God from Man*), manuscript of a conference, Pamplona 1998, p. 5.

✒3.

FREEDOM TO EXERCISE

THERE IS A SCENE THAT RECURS often in literature, art, and film: on the summit of a mountain someone lies on the grass contemplating the sky and the clouds while caressed by a gentle breeze. This is the classic image of a free man. But beyond passive contemplation, we are called to exercise our freedom by getting up, choosing a path, and setting a course for our lives.

DIRECTING ONESELF

Freedom is the capacity to direct oneself. What use is it, however, if one is afraid to make decisions? Lying in a meadow may be pleasant—or lounging in a hammock, or rocking in a rocking chair—but if you do only that day after day, you make minimal use of your freedom and will probably never succeed in becoming who you are meant to be. When you avoid taking specific and binding decisions, you let yourself be carried along by circumstances rather than being the architect of your own life. Then it will be others who decide for you, while time passes inexorably. . . . Popular wisdom and General von Moltke, a

Prussian military genius, concur that no decision is worse than the decision not to decide.

Man shows the greatness of his freedom by transforming reality. He is master of himself and, as a consequence, master of the manifestations and actions guided ultimately by his will. He has the capacity to make plans, map out projects, and provide for the future according to his own convictions.

In principle, everyone has certain general ideas about life, even though he or she may not consciously reflect on them. Each one of us has some life project, whether rich or poor, deep or superficial. Its elements include family and profession, culture and politics, moral principles and religious beliefs.

It is important to raise one's sight to great vistas, aim very high, and orient ourselves toward ideas worth living for. If one's only goal is an unfocused craving for money, one's life project is stunted. "Spain has become a great casino," it has been said,[1] and the same could be said of many other countries. Why is the "mass-man" not really free? What does he lack? Isn't he doing as he pleases in passing whole days playing with a machine in a bar? Isn't that an exercise of will? No doubt it is, but how minimal! Surely human beings are in this world to do something more important.

The key question is: What am I using my freedom for? In the absence of a "toward which," a binding and attractive goal, one can use freedom for insignificant things. "I want beer and potato chips." Here is a trivial desire, a small and narrow aspiration. A freedom bent on satisfying immediate needs is not true human freedom, but the sort of instinctive,

---

1. The Spanish Bishops, *La conciencia cristiana ante la actual situación de nuestra sociedad,* 2nd ed. (Madrid, 1990), p. 44.

physical freedom that animals have. "If you want to know a person," says St. Augustine, "don't ask him what he thinks, but what he loves."

The measure of freedom is that toward which we direct ourselves: the greater our aspirations, the greater our freedom. What matters are the dreams that can become realities, the truths that inspire your life—the arduous, difficult, but exciting goods you have set yourself to attain. One must aim high in order to expand one's heart and mobilize one's energies. "When you want to build a ship and seek people to do the job," says an old German proverb, "don't tell them to gather materials and make complicated calculations. Open up to them a yearning for the boundless sea."

Freedom means both to direct and "to make" oneself. I make myself by my free decisions. In them I am not only the agent but also the one acted upon. Someone who decides to become a doctor will in a few years—if he pursues that decision—be a different person than if he decided to become an artist. Many things in life depend, at least in large part, on one's will: state in life, profession, friends, practice of the faith.

INFLUENCES ON THE WILL

But freedom is not expressed only through the will. It is also intimately related to one's understanding: I love what I know and consider good; I reject what I know and consider bad. So, for instance, I write a letter to a friend if I know, or at least suppose, that he or she is expecting it and will receive it with pleasure. Behavior similarly is influenced by feelings. I may write the letter to communicate a great joy or get something off my chest. Or perhaps some external need leads me to write the letter: I need to transmit important information or communicate something someone needs to know. So although I don't feel like it, I write the letter.[2]

The Importance of the Intellect

Intellect and will are faculties that interact in a reciprocal manner. Someone is only excited about a book if he has read it, and he will only read it if he is interested in its contents.[3]

Normally, a free act follows the information presented to the understanding. It is important that this information be true, not marred by ignorance and error. For instance, when deciding whether to attend a literary conference, I need to know that it will actually take place, what the exact subject will be, and where and when it will be held. It is important that the information I acquire be true. If I decide to participate on June 17 in a conference in Paris, and this conference actually took place May 20 in Seville, I'm in for a disappointment. It would be even worse if I were to confuse poisonous mushrooms for edible ones. My false information could lead me to get sick and die!

To get to the truth of something, the will in some way "pushes" the understanding. Since I fear that the mushrooms might be poisonous, I do well to consult a reference book and ask people who know the secrets of the forest. (The will "leads" the understanding to act.) It could also be that the mushrooms seem so appetizing that I eat them at once, not bothering to gather more information because it seems

---

2. I speak this way to explain a complex reality as clearly as possible. However, we need to keep in mind that it is always *the person* who thinks and decides and carries out the action. It is not the intellect but the man or woman who understands.

3. In fact, both intellect and will have universal objects that mutually include each other: what is true is an aspect of the universal good, and the good is a particular sense of truth. The will does not move us to love unless the intellect first proposes a fitting object. Nor will the intellect understand anything unless moved to this act by the will.

superfluous and bothersome to me at the moment. (In this case, the will "puts the brakes on" the act of understanding.)

The will can impede the operation of the intellect in many areas. In line with popular lifestyles, people consciously or unconsciously avoid getting to the bottom of things, hold back their thoughts from reaching that troublesome point where their comfort might be called into question. They decide simply to *enjoy themselves as much as they can*. And yet they remain very far from achieving that. Sooner or later boredom or sickness sets in, or they suffer failure or rejection. There is no escaping frustration. "The drama lies in the fact that we can never become drunk enough," confesses André Gide in his diary.[4] Often it is precisely those who seek immediate pleasure who are unable really to enjoy themselves, because they have within them a kind of disgust for their own lives.

Others center everything on *work*. They want to use their practical, artistic, intellectual, or social talents to contribute to the welfare of their families and the progress of the world, or they simply seek a bit of esteem, applause, and success. Centered as they are on development and progress, our competitive societies invite us to think of life as a contest that must be won. Yet in the end we reach the same dead end. What happens when we can't work and become a burden for others? Work and applause end, not life— and life has lost its meaning.

There are times when a person can't help sensing the folly of closing his eyes to the question of life's ultimate reason. Resignation or bitterness is unavoidable unless one manages to live in a very superficial manner. Why get up every morning if someday everything will end? Why build

---

4. André Gide, *Journal 1889–1939* (Paris, 1948), p. 89.

a house and start a family if two hundred years from now neither house nor family will exist? These are pressing questions everyone must settle one way or another. No one can fully realize himself or herself by acting contrary to the truth of his or her being. "I must base myself on an indisputable truth," said Nietzsche. "Only then can I become happy."[5]

Unless the ultimate meaning of life is located in eternity, it cannot satisfy us fully; all that we do will be fundamentally absurd. We will be acting in a vacuum, and life will become a disoriented adventure. A well-known philosopher expresses it simply: "Only if I believe in God can I be fully certain that my life has meaning."[6]

Every man must follow the truth that he himself has encountered through meditation, reading, dialogue—and, above all, by listening to God's voice within him.[7] One's internal logic falls apart if one fails to act by it.[8] On the other hand, we must also accept the help that many other people—of all classes and conditions—can offer. If we ourselves are our only source of questions and ideas, we are in danger of never being challenged and losing the clarity of our thought.

It has been said that freedom—considered as the property of possessing within ourselves the principle of our action—is

---

5. See Friedrich Nietzsche, *Die Unschuld des Werdens* (posthumous) (Leipzig, 1930), p. 84.

6. See Ludwig Wittgenstein, *Tagebücher 1914–1916*, in *Schriften* I (Frankfurt, 1960), pp. 166ff. Wittgenstein had a certain mystical vision of life's meaning.

7. See Joseph Ratzinger (Benedict XVI), *Truth, Values, Power: Litmus Tests for a Pluralist Society* (San Francisco, 1995), p. 53 (Spanish edition).

"Man can see the truth of God in the depths of his creaturely being. . . . He only ceases to see when he does not want to see, that is to say *because* he does not want to see. . . . Not seeing the flashing light is a result of having voluntarily turned one's gaze away from something that *we do not want to see*."

8. See Vatican II, Declaration *Dignitatis Humanae* (*DH*), 1 and 3.

a joint project of intellect and will.[9] It has its root in the intellect, which knows the world,[10] while its proper subject is the will, which is directed toward the world that is known. Since it is the will that moves our faculties to act, our decisions about free acts, in the end, fall back upon the will.

The Dynamic of Feelings

What do feelings have to do with freedom? They belong to human nature, as do the understanding and the will.[11] We are not merely spiritual beings; we have a body and a "heart,"[12] which is the center of all our affectivity, a person's most tender, most interior, most secret sphere. The feelings can perfect freedom. If they are lacking, action is not integrated or mature, and we do not develop completely.

Dietrich von Hildebrand lamented the fact that the heart does not have its own place in philosophy. The intellect and the will often have been studied without taking into account the rich world of feelings, placing one at risk of theorizing about reality without actually examining it. Nevertheless, this author explains: "Shouldn't the fact that it is precisely the heart of Jesus, not his intellect or his will, that is the object of a specific devotion, lead one to a deeper appreciation of the nature of the heart and, consequently, a revision of one's attitude toward the affective

---

9. See Thomas Aquinas, *Summa Theologiae*, q.1, a.1, c.: "*Libertas est . . . facultas voluntatis et rationis.*"

10. See Aquinas, *De Veritate*, 24, 2.

11. By the term *feelings* I refer to the central life of the affections and understand emotions, passions, and motivations as the particular modalities of feeling. *Emotions* are characterized by their sudden appearance; they always include a physical change; they can reach a great intensity, but are temporary. *Passions* are intense and more persistent; and *motivations* have a special capacity to propel life toward the future.

12. I use the term heart as a synonym for "feelings," not as a human faculty over and above intellect and will.

sphere?"[13] Hildebrand uncovers the superficiality of indifference to affectivity, false "sobriety," exaggerated emphasis on the will, and pseudo-objectivity in saying: "To have a heart capable of loving, a heart which can know anxiety and suffering, which can be afflicted and moved, is the most typical characteristic of human nature."[14]

Insensitivity is a genuine deficiency. Thomas Aquinas considered it not only a defect but also a vice.[15] The inability to enjoy the good things of life and excessively cold, dry behavior could well have a pathological origin.[16]

The feelings are based on impulses (instincts, appetites, tendencies). These impulses can also be observed in animals. They are traditionally divided into two large groups: those pertaining to *desire,* or "the tendency toward a good," and those pertaining to *struggle* to attain this good.[17] Unlike the animals, however, man is conscious of his impulses and can moderate them to some degree.

The affective sphere includes experiences at very different levels. These range from corporal sensations (a headache, thirst) to "psychic" feelings (for example, fatigue, certain depressions, or the good humor one feels after a glass of wine). But a person's affective life cannot be limited to these experiences. Man is also capable of "spiritual feelings"[18]—noble enthusiasm, profound joy, grief, contrition, compassion, and

---

13. Dietrich von Hildebrand, *El corazón. Un analisis de la afectividad humana y divina (The Heart: An Analysis of Human and Divine Affectivity)* (Madrid, 1997), p. 26.

14. Ibid., p. 15.

15. Aquinas, *Summa Theologiae* II-II, q. 142, a.1; q.153, a3, ad 3.

16. Physical conditions have a role in the arousal of feelings; hence the influence of drugs on affectivity.

17. Traditionally one speaks of the "concupiscible appetite" and the "irascible appetite."

18. See "Prologue" in Von Hildebrand, *El Corazon,* cit., pp. 9–11.

other affections that stir the heart. These feelings can enkindle love or give rise to crushing sorrow. A sensible component and a higher affectivity are ordinarily present in feelings.

Of course, feelings can obscure the truth. A man may put obstacles in the way of understanding or set out on the wrong path in response to the promptings of feeling. In the example cited earlier, I don't want to find out whether the mushrooms are dangerous because I *very much want* to eat them now. Or I do not want to know the truth about something for fear of the consequences. It is necessary to take seriously all affective experiences, accept them, identify them, and order them properly. Normally, one can freely will to correct feelings that do not correspond to one's plan of life, at least to the extent of preventing them from influencing one's behavior. While the arousal of feelings cannot be avoided directly, usually we can choose whether or not to do what the feelings urge us to do. Someone who lives in accord with his interior order lives freely: he is not dominated by passing situations that are here today and gone tomorrow. Freedom does not depend essentially on feelings, although feelings can enrich freedom. When a feeling is prolonged, it becomes more one's own, more "personal."

The more profound, intense, and persistent the affective experience is, the more difficult it becomes for a person to be directed by the will. A man suffers a great misfortune—the death of his wife, for example. He weeps, laments, reminisces; he can neither work nor eat. But, ordinarily, after a while the time comes when he can't weep anymore. This is not from a lack of loyalty toward his wife; it is a sign that he is alive. No matter how intense a particular psychic state might be, it cannot and should not be permanent. A slow process of detachment follows it, for life goes on. We cannot remain in the past or "mummify" the dead.

To remain sorrowful would block the rhythm of nature, and the relationship with the dead person could not be considered sane.

"Keeping promises to the dead, or to anyone else, is very well," said C.S. Lewis. "But I begin to see that 'respect for the wishes of the dead' is a trap."[19] This *respect* can be a form of tyranny, with one's own will concealed behind the supposed will of the dead person. There is a great danger of manipulating others with phrases like "He (or she) wanted it that way." What matters isn't what somebody may have wanted ten, twenty, or forty years ago, but what he wants *now*. If we are Christians and believe the dead person is with God, we should think he or she wants what God wants: that we go on living and be happy.

Feelings aren't ends in themselves and should not paralyze us. And "what a person feels for another is not a question of sensations, emotions, or a beating of the heart, but what one sees in *conduct*. Behavior often shows one's feelings more directly, visibly, and authentically than words."[20]

Our goal should not be the absence of feelings or always maintaining a natural cheerfulness, but rather to have feelings appropriate to the situation, and sometimes a situation calls for profound suffering. Von Hildebrand uses an example from the Old Testament. When Abraham hears God telling him to sacrifice his son Isaac, he freely says yes and puts aside his paternal feelings. But his heart must have been bleeding and full of sadness. Would he have been freer if his heart had not felt sad? "On the contrary," says von Hildebrand, "that would have been a monstrous attitude."

---

19. C.S. Lewis, *A Grief Observed* (New York: HarperOne, 1989), p. 21.
20. Ricardo Yepes Stork, *Fundamentos de antropología* (Pamplona, 1996), p. 62.

God's will required that the sacrifice of a son elicit Abraham's sorrow.[21]

Do not undervalue the importance of feelings. No one develops fully without them. Feelings can impel us forward or hold us back; they point to the future. Sometimes they seem to have a dynamic of their own. Coaches know that some days their athletes will give more and other days less. Having suffered a failure or a deception, one is discouraged, without energy. Receiving good news, one is ready to undertake great things. It is good to understand that one's present state of soul influences how one sees the world.

Experience also teaches that many impressions, though no longer conscious, have not completely disappeared but form part of the *subconscious* mind.[22] This is a realm where past impressions, desires, and feelings remain in some way active—capable of powerfully influencing our behavior. This is particularly important to take into account in explaining certain psychopathological phenomena.

The External Situation

External situations can also notably limit our freedom, but they can never exclude it completely; nor do they intervene essentially in the free act. The Romans called their children *liberi,* "the free ones," which originally meant those who were not slaves. A freeman is someone not subject to another, not required to do things he does not want to do, whom no one can prevent from doing what he wants.

For some Socratic schools and especially for the Stoics, everything "external"—society, nature, even one's own

---

21. Von Hildebrand, *El Corazon,* cit., p. 203.
22. We speak of *unconscious* in the case of an actual lack of consciousness; *subconscious,* on the other hand, suggests impressions close to consciousness.

passions, aside from the spirit—is considered in some sense oppressive. Freedom consists in "disposing of oneself." But this disposing of self is not possible unless one has freed oneself from "the exterior," the external. In the end, then, the freeman is one who is independent of others, attentive only, as Seneca said, "to the things that are within us."

Freedom is understood here as the freedom to be oneself. And for philosophers like the Neo-Platonists who equated being oneself with being able to dedicate oneself to contemplation, freedom consisted essentially in "contemplating" and rejecting action. A free person is one who sets aside "business" in order to devote himself to "leisure" (or for the Neo-Platonists, study) so as to more perfectly cultivate his personality.

This view of freedom as liberation from whatever disturbs and bothers one is easily understood today. We feel free on weekends when we can devote ourselves to leisure—normally, not studying or working but watching television, being comfortable and relaxed, without any hassles. And indeed the absence of external nuisances really can favor freedom. Someone who can't play his trumpet because the neighbors object can't "realize himself" in this way and so lacks freedom. So, too, a young person pressured to become a businessman like his father is restricted and determined by forces from outside himself.

But even though external factors can notably reduce freedom, they can't entirely remove it. Coercion—of whatever kind, arising from circumstances or other persons—does not eliminate freedom but only reduces it. A classic example illustrates this. If a tyrant forces us to perform an evil act (killing our neighbor, for example) under threat of reprisals unless we obey ("If you don't kill your neighbor, I will kill your brother"), then we are obliged to do something at the same time involuntarily (we don't want to kill) and voluntarily (we want to avoid our brother's death). But if we obey the tyrant, we act in the end with freedom (albeit minimal), inasmuch as we've made a personal choice: to save our brother's life and kill our neighbor.

Situations can support freedom or conflict with it, increase it or diminish it. But they do not essentially obstruct the free act. Thus, a person is conditioned to a certain extent by his country, society, family of birth, education, and the culture he has received, by his body, his genetic code, and nervous system, his talents, limits, and previous experiences. Yet he is free, because he possesses the ability to look beyond all these conditioning factors.

A man can be free even in prison, as many people throughout history have shown (Boethius, St. Thomas More, Dietrich Bonhoeffer, St. Maximilian Kolbe). "There is a part of you which no one can take away from you, it is yours," says one prisoner to another, in a powerful dialogue occurring in the movie *Sueños de libertad* (Dreams of Freedom). A man can also be free in a totalitarian state. He can continue to hold a belief, a desire, or a love in the depths of his soul even though its total abolition is externally decreed. Sacharov was great not only as a physicist but above all as a man, a passionate fighter for the freedom of all. For this he paid the price of suffering imposed on him by the Communist regime whose falseness and inhumanity he had revealed to the world.

❧4.

FREEDOM TO LOVE

FREEDOM, AS WE HAVE SEEN, is realized through the will, which is influenced—in a gradually distinct way—by intellect, feelings, and external situations. Now let us consider how the will acts and what its principal acts are.

Freedom often comes into play in a supermarket. The shopper confronts many wonderful things to pick up, look at, turn over, and put down again, comparing and choosing among them. In selecting, say, the tobacco he likes best, he certainly performs a free act. But having gone to the checkout counter, bought the tobacco, and pocketed it, he feels even freer. And when back home he lights up a pipe full of the tobacco, he feels happy. Here is what he wanted from the beginning.

The various acts of the will are visible in this sketch. First I choose what seems good to me, then I seek union with this good, which means that I love what I have chosen. Love is understood as a tendency toward something or someone at all levels. In this sense, I "love" a kind of food, a game, a city; I love people and I love God. Love not only *follows*, however, but in a deeper sense also precedes every choice. The man who buys tobacco already has an idea (at least a vague one) of what he does and doesn't want to buy.

But when the choice has been made, his love is intensified, and in the achievement of union with the loved good (smoking the pipe), happiness results.

Thus one can say that freedom tends toward happiness and is principally exercised in two acts: the choice and the love. Let's look more closely at these three realities: the spontaneous desire to be happy, the choice, and the love.

THE SPONTANEOUS DESIRE TO BE HAPPY

Everyone wants to be happy; people want their lives to be realized in a full, thorough way, and they rejoice when they attain what they aspire to. When I am with someone I love, I am happy. When I pass a test for which I've studied hard, I also am happy, though in a different way. Full happiness requires fullness of development in all human dimensions. That includes the affective sphere, since the only way to experience happiness, whatever its source, is to feel it. If someone only *desires* to be happy or knows with his intellect that he *should consider himself* happy, then he isn't truly happy yet. Happiness can only be experienced with the heart. There is in us an "original love" (Thomas Aquinas) or "intimate impulse" (Bl. John Paul II) tending toward fullness.[1] We incline spontaneously toward what we consider good, under any aspect and in any degree.

Someone might ask why this natural tendency exists in the depths of one's heart. Why do we feel a desire to develop ourselves? Why do we want to be happy? We see here an expression of our condition as creature. Man indeed is a cause of himself, but not his final cause. His nature, being created, has an end or purpose: man is ordered to happiness

---

1. *Veritatis Splendor*, 7.

in the love of God. And being so ordered, man seeks this satisfaction in all his actions. God in some way continually attracts him and calls him to himself. In one way or another, although often unconscious, he is always moved by the love of God, identified with the desire for full happiness. The famous words of St. Augustine, "You have made us for yourself, O Lord, and our hearts are restless until they rest in you," are as timely now as ever.

Man acts in all aspects of life to attain ends that he recognizes as good. He studies a profession to get a job; he works to earn money; he saves to build a house; he builds the house to start a family. . . . The ends may be partial, intermediate, even less than human, but they give meaning to his actions. But although man seeks happiness in all these ways, it is not to be found in any limited good. The object of the will is universal; by its very nature, it tends to transcend itself; it is directed at something beyond, toward the infinite.[2]

Here, though, someone might raise an objection: If our ultimate end is inscribed in our nature, we are not free to choose it. And that is partly true. Human freedom is not absolute. It lies in discovering, accepting, and loving our reality as creatures—in fact, in seeking and loving God, which brings full happiness with it.

If one tries to create other ends, giving man a power that he does not essentially possess, there is an appearance of increasing freedom but in reality freedom decreases by eliminating its depth and beauty. Freedom, in its core, does

---

2. That man "transcends" himself has been observed by various philosophers. Some contemporary thinkers conceive the *terminus ad quem* of transcendence as a future being not comparable to what we actually know as man: the "superman" according to Nietzsche; the "man of the new society" according to Marx. In these cases, "transcendence" remains in the immanent, in the life we now experience.

not consist in choosing among various possibilities. The ultimate end is a given: the possession of Love itself, which infinitely exceeds all created goods man can imagine. Someone who understands what this end is and contemplates the divine mystery sees that this does not limit his freedom, for he cannot aspire to anything more. This conviction gives life unfathomable richness and infinite possibilities.

Although man pursues happiness in everything he does, what he seeks, consciously or unconsciously, is God, which means complete happiness. Created goods, no matter how lofty, cannot completely satisfy him, and making gods of them, taking them as ends in themselves, will soon be seen for the deception it is. So, for instance, the attainment of some professional goal may be experienced as a hollow victory, far less than it had seemed to promise, and perhaps too costly in the end. Unless man can raise his aspirations, profound frustration will be in store for him. Nor is it enough simply to seek some higher professional goal, since that only postpones facing up to the problem and guarantees its recurrence. The more one seeks self-fulfillment in limited things, the less one will attain it. That can only happen by aiming higher: seeking complete happiness in unlimited Love, in God, and, in the light of God, recognizing the limitations of all the goods around us. Then, forgetting one's own fulfillment, one paradoxically finds it definitively in God.

If I continually seek joys that must be given to me by other persons or things, I will never know happiness. The more one talks about self-fulfillment, the less one attains it. The result can even be contrary to the one desired: lack of naturalness and self-centeredness. This appears to be one of the ailments of our day. The numerous therapies offered are still worse: the absence of self-fulfillment isn't remedied by speaking at length about it, for that would be like rushing around with fire extinguishers in the face of a flood or having everyone go to the same side of a sinking boat. The solution lies elsewhere, in orienting us, gently, to a higher goal than any achievable in this world. To encounter God is to encounter the greatest fullness, though not by anything we do.

Living with God is a liberating experience, like crossing the Red Sea, escaping from slavery to freedom.[3] One has a new consciousness of oneself; one feels a great relief and has a love corresponding to his or her heart's deepest desires. We are not satisfied with passing solutions. We want to live not a hundred years but forever, to be happy not just a little bit but entirely. Communion with Christ is the only way. "How is it then that I seek you, Lord? Because in seeking you, my God, I am seeking a happy life."[4]

CHOICE

The final end of man encompasses both the love of God and one's own happiness. The two aspects are inseparable: happiness consists, in the long run, in loving God, and when one has done this, one is happy.[5]

Of these two aspects of his single end, however, a man is immediately conscious only of the second. While by nature he necessarily tends to happiness in all that he does, because of the limitations of nature he doesn't necessarily tend toward God, the only good that can satisfy him completely. The primordial love (the spontaneous, natural tendency) aims naturally toward the final goal (the good, happiness) in general, but it does not specifically refer directly to God, the final end.

---

3. See Mt 17:26.
4. St. Augustine, *Confessions*, X, 20. See *CCC*, 1718.
5. See *Gaudium et Spes*, 19.

The reason lies in the fact that every act of the will must proceed from something known by the intellect. Thus, to love God explicitly, one must know him. But in this life man does not have any immediate evidence of God's existence; this goal, a given for him, entirely transcends him.

Our understanding cannot know God in all of his richness, and so it cannot present this knowledge of God to the will as the absolute good. As a result, the will lacks a necessary and specific orientation toward its true ultimate end. Thus, a real choice is required, and because of the imperfection of our nature, there is a possibility of rejecting God.

We have to *choose* the final end precisely because we do not see it clearly. If we saw God as he is, we would see that there is nothing comparable to him, and we would love him without needing to choose. That would be to love him with absolute necessity and absolute freedom, as the blessed in heaven do, free yet unable to choose between what is bad in preference to what is good. Choice is a consequence of our limitation, our finite condition in the face of God's infinity.

That we must make a real choice in regard to the final end implies the possibility of rejecting it. This is the decisive choice of our life, by which we realize or frustrate our spontaneous inclination toward the good. In the end, it is a choice between love of God and love of self, since man cannot find definitive rest in any creature. If he does not aspire to God, he turns to *himself* and makes himself (consciously or unconsciously) the ultimate goal of his life.[6]

Although people don't think constantly about their ultimate end, it is always present as the intention of their wills, just as the end of a journey orients every step the traveler takes even though he doesn't think about it constantly. We

---

6. See *Veritatis Splendor,* 39.

must choose means in view of the end, and some of these will have a closer relationship to the goal than others. For example, someone who wants to be a piano teacher must study music, with a specialization in piano; he may study psychology in order to understand his future students better; perhaps he will study physics to understand the mechanism of the instruments. An end clearly known supplies a clear criterion for the choice of means.

Insofar as he is the highest good, God includes and infinitely exceeds all particular goods. As the ultimate end of man, human beings can reach him by many very different paths that may even appear to be opposed to one another. For example, some find their path in marriage, others outside of it. God is infinite, and virtually infinite are the ways in which he can be known and loved.

Every situation can lead to God, but not all situations can lead to a particular good. Partial goals direct life toward specific situations that exclude other partial goals. Ordinarily, one can't be both a professional violinist and a professional politician. Choices have consequences that affect future choices, little by little shaping a unique and unmistakable life story.

Freedom is realized and perfected in directing oneself toward a realizable good. More important than having numerous possibilities from which to choose is reaching the end. If you want to visit a friend for the first time, you need to be told the way to his house so you don't have to waste time looking for the street. Rather than being a limitation on your freedom, taking a direct route to your friend's house is a sign of perfection. Nor is freedom reduced even if there is only one possible way of attaining the goal. If your friend lives on the other side of a river, you must cross the river to reach his house. No one is less free because he takes the necessary path to a goal he or she desires. This is why choice is only a secondary act of freedom; the primordial act is love.

LOVE

Countless songs and poems express the idea that love and freedom are intimately joined. Someone who loves feels free and fulfilled, and the greater the love, the greater the freedom he feels.[7] The person may dance in the rain, embrace his worst enemy, send a bouquet of flowers to a bad-tempered secretary, and throw a party, even though there's only lemonade in the pantry. He's happy, and he wants everyone to share his joy.

This is why those who love God—the saints—are the most original of all men. Accustomed to going against the stream, they easily free themselves of conventional attachments if a higher value requires it and boldly commit themselves to whatever God asks of them. Acting with freedom of spirit, they are reminded every day that God doesn't suppress life but gives it. "Now I only love you, I only follow you, I am ready only to serve you," exclaims St. Augustine, "because only you rule with justice; I desire to be something of yours."[8]

On the other hand, others flee from love. Neither heeding another's call nor calling anyone themselves, they remain locked in themselves, prisoners of narrowed hearts. Having only their twisted desires, sooner or later they grow frustrated. "Man and woman cannot live without love. If they

---

7. Aquinas, *In III Sent.*: "*Quanta aliquis plus habet de caritate, plus habet de libertate.*" d. 29, q. 1, a. 8.
8. St. Augustine, *Soliloqui* I, 1, 5: *PL* 32, 872.

do, they remain beings incomprehensible to themselves; their life is deprived of meaning if it is not revealed to them by love, if they do not experience it and make it their own, if they do not participate fully in it."[9]

Love is the key to freedom.[10] By it we are reborn to a more beautiful life, in which we see the world with more depth and beauty, like a country landscape seen at sunset where, more than just seeing meadows, hills, houses, and sun, we see everything bathed in the setting sun's light. To love is to experience a joyful consent to all of reality. Chesterton spoke of his "almost mystical conviction" that there was a miracle behind everything that existed. Everything bears a divine stamp, and one who discovers it is happy and gives thanks to the Creator.[11]

Loving God leads us to be interiorly free and to love the world as God loves it: "Without you, a tree would cease to be one; without you, nothing would be what it is."[12]

Needing Love

C.S. Lewis distinguished between love that is given, which moves a man to work for the good of society, to make plans and save for tomorrow with a view to the welfare of his family, and love of necessity, which propels a lonely, frightened child into its mother's arms.[13] Let's not downplay this needy love, which is the basis of many aspirations and human relationships. The primordial love that is a spontaneous movement

---

9. Bl. John Paul II, encyclical *Redemptor Hominis*, 26.

10. Christian freedom is a freedom for love, freedom from all self-induced anxiety, all imprisonment in oneself and one's own desires. Love for God and for neighbor is "the fulfillment of the law" (Rom 13:10).

11. See Maisie Ward, *Gilbert Keith Chesterton* (London–New York, 1943).

12. Giorgio Caproni, *A Rina*, in idem, *L'opera in versi* (Milan, 1998), p. 91.

13. See C.S. Lewis, *The Four Loves* (Orlando, FL: Harcourt Brace & Co., 1991), p. 1.

toward the good is, in the first place, a matter of necessity. We need others physically, affectively, and spiritually. Such love should not be dismissed as mere egoism. No one calls a child an egoist for turning to its mother for consolation or an adult for seeking out a friend to escape loneliness or have a conversation. "Where Need-love is felt there may be reasons for denying or totally mortifying it; but not to feel it is in general the mark of the cold egoist. Since we do in reality need one another . . . then the failure of this need to appear as Need-love in consciousness . . . is a bad spiritual symptom; just as lack of appetite is a bad medical symptom because men do really need food."

Above all, love of God is to a great extent needy-love, because (continues Lewis) "our whole being by its very nature is one vast need."[14] The closer we are to God, the more we see our neediness and become "jolly beggars."[15] Thus, one can understand something Nietzsche said in a poem: "I do not know the joy of one who receives."[16]

The closer we are to God, the more we become like him, and the easier it is to realize gift-love with others. In this way one reflects divine love, which is always generous and untiring in giving. A person capable of gift-love is so free that he can also love those whom he would naturally reject, whose presence he would spontaneously avoid: the disagreeable, the proud, bickerers, and egoists. Finally, God empowers man to have a gift-love toward himself. Though obviously we cannot give anything to God that isn't already his, we can give him something that God previously has given us: the capacity to love, our heart. This freedom that

---

14. See ibid., p. 3.
15. Ibid., p. 131.
16. Nietzsche, *Zarathustra*, in *Hauptwerke* I (Leipzig, 1939), p. 113.

God has given us as a natural gift at the beginning of our life reaches its highest fulfillment when we give it back to our Creator.

"My freedom for You" doesn't mean that we annul our freedom and renounce it, which would be both unworthy and impossible. Precisely because of our humanity, we can never live without freedom; we cannot conceal our own being (a gift of God) even to reach God. "My freedom for You" does not destroy freedom but energizes it: desiring to live with God and do what he tells me, I let him enter my life.

In loving—a free act par excellence—one puts into play one's independence; the stronger one's volition, the more one is attached to the other person and the stronger is the bond. But the bond is voluntary, and what resembles loss of freedom is actually its highest expression. Our relationship with God places us in contact with the source of power within us. Only someone truly in command of his or her acts can give this dominion to another and maintain that commitment. Love desires to commit itself, to surrender itself. Freedom is the greatest gift in the natural sphere, and surrendering oneself for love is its most noble exercise.[17]

But love of God is not a replacement for love of others. It is dangerous to impose on someone a duty of rooting himself in something beyond earthly love when the person's real problem is his inability of getting out of himself and thinking of others. A modern philosopher has said of certain Christians: "They don't love anyone; therefore they think that they love God."

---

17. Since Christian freedom and happiness are inseparably united, it is a mistake to say that "emancipating one from religious servitude makes men freer, but not happier." Mario Vargas Llosa, *Desafíos a la libertad* (Madrid, 1994), p. 24.

Like money, freedom must be invested or else, instead of generating wealth, it stagnates. True, any earthly love can be "disordered," lacking its end, but "disordered" is not the same as "not cautious enough" or "too great." The issue isn't how much one loves (and it's probably impossible to love a person "too much").[18] "We may love him too much *in proportion* to our love for God; but it is the smallness of our love for God, not the greatness of our love for the man, that constitutes the inordinacy."[19] St. Augustine says: "I don't say that you shouldn't love your wife, but that you should love Christ *more.*"[20]

In short, you are called to love God and others with your whole heart.[21] In this way, you shall realize your freedom completely and someday, usually after many detours, arrive at its fulfillment.

Being Capable of Friendship

The new man, the one who is free, enjoys being with others: open, cheerful, affectionate, he is their friend.

The art of loving is not to be confused with setting new records as in some sporting event. Nor is it enough to give "things" to the person one loves. Rather, we must give something of our very selves, of our own life, of what is living in us, by sharing joys and pains, enthusiasms and failures, experiences and plans for the future—in a word,

---

18. See Aquinas, *Summa Theologiae* I, q. 65, a. 1, ad 3: "In themselves, creatures do not separate us from God, rather they lead us to Him. . . . If in some cases they separate us from God, the fault is with those who do not make proper use of them."

19. See Lewis, *The Four Loves*, cit., p. 122.

20. St. Augustine cited in Von Hildebrand, *El Corazon*, cit., p. 210.

21. "The divine image is present in every man. It shines forth in the communion of persons, in the likeness of the union of the divine persons among themselves." *CCC*, 1702.

giving of ourselves, offering friendship. Some people throw themselves feverishly into social welfare work, yet without ever having a genuine encounter with another person in which each shows himself to the other as he really is.

Sincere contact with others increases our vitality: we experience more and draw more from it. C.S. Lewis speaks of his experiences of being with friends as "golden." After hiking for a day, he came with four or five friends to an inn where they took off their wet, dirty shoes and sat, feet extended, before a cheery fireplace with a glass at hand. It seemed as if the world had opened up before them as they spoke freely, as equals, with a sincerity that you only have among friends.[22]

A friend is someone we like to be with, someone with whom we can be ourselves, who accepts those same contradictions in us that move others to judge us badly. Even when everything goes wrong, friendship can encourage and sustain, strengthen us, and give us security and freedom.

A person with friends from other political parties, other professions, other religions, and other nationalities, is a happy man. A limitless sea is open to him. Dealing with and loving the most varied people expands one's heart, deepens one's knowledge of the human condition, and adds nuance to one's judgments of complex situations. Yet some people remain in closed environments, preferring greenhouse air to the harsh atmosphere of the street. Irreproachable though their lives may be, they sometimes may exhibit deplorable childishness—unaware of the struggles and sufferings of others, and so ignorant of the human heart that they know only two colors: black and white; and two kinds of people: sinners and martyrs who die with a song on their lips.

---

22. See Lewis, *The Four Loves,* cit., p. 72.

Existing for Others

A free person also knows how to liberate others. He discovers and awakens the life of those around him, helping each to grow at his own pace.

It is important to find the right way of relating to each person according to his or her character and particular circumstances in the awareness that each one is different. "Every human being is an individual person and therefore I cannot program *a priori* a certain type of relationship that could be applied to everyone, but I must, so to speak, learn it anew in every case."[23] Love places everyone first; no one is second.

Each person is important and sacred, no matter what his failings and errors, his weaknesses, or his past life. If the last will be first in Christ's kingdom, we must respect the blade of grass more than the orchid, the drop of dew more than the waterfall—we must ask God to take off our blinders.

Some speak of an "asceticism of human relations"[24] that consists of giving space to the other so that he can develop in his own way—not passing judgment on somebody when everyone else is judging him, not scorning or rejecting him, and seeing his failings "with the eyes of a friend."[25]

In moments of discouragement, weakness, or distress, it is tremendously important to encounter a person who understands, who does not quarrel, who does not coldly classify one, but who gives consolation and relief.[26] The

23. Bl. John Paul II, *Rise, Let Us Be On Our Way* (New York, 2004), pp. 65–66; see p. 102. Idem, Apostolic letter *Novo Millennium Ineunte:* "Now is the time for a new 'creativity' in charity," no. 50.

24. See Heribert Gault, "*Askese der Beziehung*," in *Lebendige Seelsorge* 35 (1984), p. 40.

25. Romano Guardini, *Tugenden, Meditationen über Gestalten sittlichen Lebens* (Mainz-Paderborn, 1987), (third ed.), p. 87.

26. Bl. John Paul II, *Rise, Let Us Be On Our Way:* "I always follow this principle: I welcome everyone as a person sent to me and entrusted to me by Christ," p. 67.

"asceticism" can be seen in the capacity to listen, which moves us to make the effort to engage others deeply, not satisfied merely with what they say but striving to hear what they *want* to say—not just words but messages. To listen is charity. At times it is the vocation of being a wastebasket or garbage can. The scarcity of such listening "wastebaskets" is why so many people are lonely: they are oppressed by experiences they cannot share with anyone.

Often, too, people who come to you for advice go away happy without even hearing your answer. It wasn't advice they wanted, but your silence, your patience, and the chance to vent their feelings.

We need to get rid of the pride we take in giving instructions and being right, which so often prevents us from truly hearing others. Someone who admits his own weakness can encourage others and allow them to grow, but someone who has all the answers can paralyze those around him. "Don't speak if you aren't sure what you're going to say is more beautiful than silence" is a pithy piece of folk wisdom.

A patient person knows how to live by somebody else's time, how to wait for the right moment to point out a possible fault—to that individual alone, not to someone else. An old monk of the desert gave a young man who wanted to follow him this golden rule: "Eat when you are hungry; drink when you are thirsty; sleep when you are tired. But never speak badly of anyone. This is how you will find salvation."

Loving others doesn't mean simply doing things for them, but trusting in the life that's in them; it means understanding them, with their more or less appropriate reactions, their fears, and their hopes. It means showing them that they are unique and worthy of attention, helping them accept their own worth, their own beauty, the light hidden in them, the meaning of their life. It means communicating to others the joy that you feel in being with them.

Someone who experiences being loved for what he is, with no need to show himself competent or interesting, feels secure in the presence of the other; the masks and barriers behind which he has hidden disappear. It's no longer necessary to flaunt or conceal anything or to protect himself. A person who acquires the freedom to be himself grows cheerful and likeable. There springs up in him a new life, enabling him to mature and grow. Perhaps someone who has been far removed from any spiritual life may once more open himself to God.

People today aren't converted just by reading treatises about God or hearing erudite lectures about him. Like Thomas, the doubting apostle, people today desire to put their searching hands into the open heart of the Church.

❧ 5.

OBEYING GOD:
THE SOURCE OF FREEDOM

A PERSON CAN ONLY BE FREE IF HE wants to be and if he is prepared to get in touch with his interior truth. Not just any truth makes us free,[1] but the truth about ourselves, which is none other than what God had in mind for us when he pronounced our names.

Other truths we learn in the course of life can be very interesting. They may even be of great service to others. But unless I know who I am and who I can become, I am like the captain of a ship sailing with no course and navigating by whim, who only stumbles on sunken treasure by accident.

Even worse is to build one's life on falsehoods, on the appearance of a brilliant exterior ever attentive to what others say. This ship lacks a solid structure; it has holes in the hull, and sooner or later will sink.

WALKING IN THE TRUTH

Only the truth that is mine makes me free. This is a costly good, acquired progressively insofar as one enters into it.

---

1. Cf. Jn 8:32.

It demands commitment—participation and placing myself at risk. The person I am, whom God has always wanted, has a unique face and an unmistakable task in this world. Therefore, I mustn't think as everyone else thinks and act as everyone else acts only because "everybody else" does. Does God want this from me? Here is an important question that I mustn't suppress, uncomfortable though it may be. I must get used to facing it, at least in certain important moments of my life. Even formulating the question may require effort, especially at first, although I'll soon realize it is worth facing with courage. The answer may lead me to change course and sail against the current. Yet at the same time I shall have the joyful certainty that I am approaching, little by little, a wonderful harbor. To reach it, I am ready to brave any danger on the high seas.

When one knows that the trip will end well, the events of life can be seen as a beautiful adventure or a fascinating sport. For example, with waterskiing you put on the right kind of skis, grasp a long rope tied to a motorboat, and, as the boat picks up speed, try not to lose your balance. What a joy to feel the wind and water in your face, to see the great waves rising on either side! Despite all the "risks," you know that in the end you'll emerge safe and sound from the water.

But without that link to a boat that will carry you to dry land, it would be a completely different experience. The wind and waves would be terrifying enemies. You would feel the panic that comes from being underwater—and not without reason, since drowning would be a real danger. You wouldn't have the assurance of the skier, who, although being pulled at great speed, knows that he will not be abandoned in the middle of the ocean but will be brought safely to the shore.

A Christian is not afraid of life or death. Whatever happens, happiness in his true homeland awaits him at the end. To reach it, he is ready to struggle and suffer. Usually he will have a fundamental serenity in doing this, arising from the conviction of being on the right path. He knows that the only real danger lies in going astray, leaving the path, betraying his own truth, and losing contact with himself.

Besides, a Christian is never alone. He has allowed Christ to enter his life. God himself is steering his boat, letting him know where he must go and how to navigate. Like the interior life as a whole, freedom too has an essentially dialogical character: Myself face to face with God.

The experience of Christ's loving closeness frees us to know the truth ever more clearly. "The Lord, my God, lightens my darkness,"[2] sings the psalmist. Actually, since God is the highest truth, someone united to him can only be a realist.[3] Seeing the world as it is, with its lights and shadows, one does not create illusions or have false ideas about it. One also sees oneself as one is and as one ought to be. A person gradually understands why he or she is born and what God expects of him or her.

The better you understand your mission on earth, the stronger you become, because your freedom to overcome obstacles grows.

CONSCIENCE

The voice of God in us is traditionally called conscience. The term, which comes from the Latin, means "to know with"—in this case, to know with God what I should do at

2. Ps 17:28.
3. See Jn 14:6.

each moment to realize his plan for me.[4] It is a participation in divine wisdom itself.

Conscience gives human beings an extraordinary dignity.[5] It's like a personal hotline to God, worth more than any command or counsel from others. Conscience is "the first of all of the vicars of Christ."[6] Who could presume to say his words are more important than what God directly tells me?

Here we find ourselves at the core of the human heart—for many thinkers, the greatest thing in the world. "In conscience, man is alone with the greatest or the worst of himself, and through conscience . . . he is above all alone with God."[7]

Through conscience—that is, through our most intimate thoughts and feelings—God speaks to us, instructs us, and teaches us to live in conformity with our true being. Hearing his voice and being disposed to heed it does not reduce our creativity or our talents. On the contrary, it's then that we attain true originality. God communicates different things to each of us. Everyone is for him an only son or daughter. Therefore, we can enrich others, for we all have something others do not have; we all can learn from those around us.

Following One's Conscience

Everyone should act in a manner consistent with what conscience tells him.[8] God infuses a light in the intellect,

---

4. See *Dominum et Vivificantem* (no. 54): "God is in the depths of your being as a thought, conscience, heart; it is a psychological and ontological reality."

5. The conscience is the most secret part of the person, where God speaks and each person decides his own destiny. See *Gaudium et Spes* 14; 26; 41 and 73.

6. CCC, 1778.

7. J. Morales, *La fidelidad*, 2nd ed. (Madrid, 2004), p. 130.

8. See Aquinas, *Summa Theologiae*, I-II, q. 93, a. 3, ad 2.

and unless we voluntarily extinguish it, it can point to what is good without needing any special help from without.[9] Indeed, one *should not* follow the advice of others when it contradicts what, in the depths of one's heart, one considers to be good.

The moral life is based, then, on the principle of a "just autonomy" of man, who possesses within himself the law received from the Creator and is the personal subject of his actions.[10] He has an obligation to follow faithfully the dictates of his conscience, on the model of Cardinal Newman, who could affirm at the end of his long life, "I have never sinned against the light."[11]

Only by acting in this way will one be united to God and correspond to his plan for one's life. Therefore, no one can force another to act against his convictions or prevent another from acting according to them, within due limits of a just public order.[12]

Seen from another perspective, no one should place responsibility for his own actions upon others. If he does, he loses the dignity of a free son and makes himself the slave of a master. "He who acts spontaneously acts freely. But he who receives his impulse from another, does not act freely."[13] Functionaries of political regimes, brought to jus-

---

9. See idem, *In dua praecepta caritatis et in decem legis praecepta. Prologus: Opuscula theological*, II, no. 1129.

10. *Gaudium et Spes*, 41.

11. John Henry Newman, cited in Ida F. Görres, *Der Geopferte. Ein anderer Blick auf John Henry Newman* (Vallendar, 2004), p. 93.

12. See *DH*, 1; 2; 3 and10. *Catechism of the Catholic Church*, 1782 and 2106. "God willed that man should be left 'in the power of his own inclination'" (Sir 15:14). . . . Man's dignity therefore requires him to act out of conscious and free choice, as moved and drawn in a personal way from within, and not by blind impulses in himself or by mere external constraint" (*Gaudium et Spes*, 17).

13. Aquinas, *In 2 Cor*, c. 3, lect 3. *In Rom*, c. 2, lect 3. *Contra Gentiles* IV, 22. *Summa Theologiae* I-II, q. 108 a. 1 ad 2.

tice for their crimes, justify murders, tortures, robbery and other evil deeds with the excuse that they were carrying out their superiors' commands.

We should grow accustomed to acting by conviction, not convention, in everyday life. This means not letting others lead us where we don't want to go or unthinkingly permitting our surroundings to seduce us. "With reason, we consider that a person has reached adulthood when he can discern on his own the difference between what is true and what is false, forming his own judgment."[14]

Forming the Conscience

One can only follow a truth that is understood. It's impossible to do things one considers absurd or harmful, at least for an extended period of time, without encountering difficulty. This principle also applies to the practice of religion. St. Thomas prudently notes: "One who avoids doing evil, not because it is evil, but because it is a command of the Lord, is not free. On the contrary, he who avoids the evil because it is evil, he is free. . . . He is not free in the sense that he is not subject to God's law, but because his interior dynamism leads him to do what the divine law prescribes."[15] As long as an adolescent doesn't know what the Mass is, the Sunday precept seems to him a burdensome formalism that he perhaps succeeds in fulfilling from a confused feeling of duty or simply because of family pressure. If, on the other hand, he understands and accepts with faith the meaning of the liturgical celebration, he will go happily to Mass, and not on Sundays only.

---

14. Bl. John Paul II, encyclical *Fides et Ratio*, 2.

15. Aquinas, *In 2 Cor*, c. 3, lect 3. *In Rom*, c. 2, lect 3. *Contra Gentiles* IV, 22. *Summa Theologiae* I-II, q. 108 a. 1 ad 2.

We also have to follow the dictates of conscience, even though it may be mistaken, when it tells us that things like eating pork or going to the theater or dancing are morally illicit.[16] If we act contrary to what our conscience tells us in such cases, we corrupt ourselves, even though the things in question are not objectively wrong.[17]

Here it becomes apparent that conscience, though "first of all the vicar of Christ" for us, is in the last resort *not* what determines the goodness or badness of actions. In fact, the autonomy of conscience is relative, since it is ordained toward the full truth and "in relation" to it.

We therefore have a grave duty to form our consciences, because their function does not consist in *creating* but *finding* truth and values.[18] Only by praying, studying, and contemplating the divine law will we remain in intimate contact with God.[19] Otherwise the words God wants to communicate to us cannot be distinguished from the voice of our egoism and pride.

Conscience can be deformed in two senses: it can be superficial and dulled, or it can be scrupulous, seeing duties where they don't exist and grossly exaggerating the demands of duty. In the first case, it is not the voice of God that is heard but only the noises generated by oneself or by others, such as a bureaucrat who sees it as his responsibil-

---

16. See Rom 14:22–23: "The faith that you have, keep between yourself and God; happy is he who has no reason to judge himself for what he approves. But he who has doubts is condemned, if he eats, because he does not act from faith; for whatever does not proceed from faith is sin."

17. Catholic theology has always considered the so-called "rights of an erroneous conscience" as fundamental, among other things, to religious freedom. See Roger Aubert, "*Le probléme de la liberté religieuse à travers L'histoire du christianisme,*" in *Scripta Theologica* (1/1969), p. 380f.

18. See *Gaudium et Spes*, 47.

19. See Ps 143[142]:10: "Teach me to do thy will."

ity simply to be the instrument of his superiors' will. His conscience is completely clean because he has never used it. He may be extremely diligent and effective, but he lives a subhuman life. Freedom was not made for the timid, who tremble in the face of its enormous responsibility and never dare to make judgments of their own.

At the other extreme are people who constantly suffer from guilty feelings for actions that, objectively, are not evil. Rather than pointing to real guilt, such feelings express a lack of clarity in their way of understanding moral precepts. So, for instance, they accuse themselves of lack of charity simply for observing defects in others.

The appropriate motto for conscience isn't "the stricter, the better" but "the truer, the better."[20] What counts is the connection with God, which gives the interior clarity we need. It not only admonishes us and leads us to avoid what is *prohibited* but above all encourages us to do *what is asked* and to undertake great things.

A DIVINE ADVENTURE

Someone accustomed to forming his or her conscience by repeatedly directing it toward the true and the good is able to really hear God in his or her heart.[21] God's advice may be demanding, his commands difficult, but they will never lead to alienation. On the contrary, if you fulfill them, you will

---

20. See Jn 18:37: "Everyone who is of the truth hears my voice."

21. In the New Testament, obedience is almost always considered as obedience to God. The New Testament also speaks, of course, of other forms of obedience to human institutions (1 Pet 2:3), but in a subordinate and less solemn manner. St. Paul speaks of obedience of *faith* (Rom 1:5; 16:26; see also Acts 6:7), of obedience to *doctrine* (Rom 6:17), of obedience to the *Gospel* (Rom 10:16; 2 Thess 1:8), of obedience to the *truth* (Gal 5:7; see also 1 Pet 1:22), of obedience to Christ (2 Cor 10:5; see also 1 Pet 1:2).

be ever more "you." Agnes Gonxha Bojaxhiu heard the call and went to India to care for the poor and sick. Had she not followed this voice, she would never have become Bl. Teresa of Calcutta. The young Angelo Giuseppe Roncalli heard the call to the priesthood; had he rejected it, we would not have known Bl. Pope John XXIII.

With the Power of the Spirit

The saints possess strength to respond from the depths of their hearts to what God asked of them. They respond to love with love, with a great availability for unforeseen ventures. "Here am I," said Abraham when God called him;[22] "Here am I," said Moses,[23] Samuel,[24] Isaiah,[25] the Virgin Mary,[26] and Jesus Christ himself, true God and true man: "Lo, I have come to do thy will."[27]

Where did they get the courage to risk their lives and surmount every obstacle in their way? Not from themselves only! They were filled with God—so much so that one could say they were immersed in him. There was in them a space only God could fill. Therefore, they saw their mission on earth and their path to heaven clearly, and they were anxious to press ahead. They wanted what God wanted. Their immense interior freedom could be seen in their prompt, even joyful readiness to fulfill the divine will.[28] "Give me someone who knows what it is to love," says St. Augustine, "and he will understand what I am saying."

---

22. Gen 22:1.
23. Ex 3:4.
24. 1 Sam 3:1ff.
25. Is 6:8.
26. Lk 1:38.
27. Heb 10:9.
28. See Ps 1:1–3.

Christ came to invite everyone to intimacy with God.[29] He wanted to pour out his grace upon all mankind. He wanted his Spirit to enter into even the least of his servants.[30] Ordinarily, together with the Father and the Son, the divine Spirit takes possession of our hearts through prayer and the sacraments. "Without the Spirit," writes St. Athanasius, "we are strangers and far from God. If, on the contrary, we participate in the Spirit, we unite ourselves to the divinity."[31] The Divine Spirit acts in the deepest part of our being, while at the same time sharing mysteriously in the response of our freedom.[32] "His activity in our souls is a *motion;* he sanctifies us by moving with the gentleness of love and with the efficacy of omnipotence all of the actions of our being. Only he can move us in that way, because only he can penetrate into the hidden sanctuary of our soul . . . hidden from the sight of all creatures. Only he can move us like that, because only he has the divine secret of touching the fonts of human activity, without those acts ceasing to be vital and *free.*"[33]

It is a mystery of love. God wants to be ours and wants us to be his. "Our most intimate acts of faith, of love and of hope, our dispositions of soul and feelings, our most personal and free resolutions—all of these irrefutable realities that are *ours,* are penetrated in such a

---

29. See *Dignitatis Humanae,* 11: Christ "bore witness to the truth, but he refused to impose the truth by force on those who spoke against it. Not by force of blows does his rule assert its claims. It is established by witnessing to the truth and by hearing the truth."

30. See Acts 2:18 and Eph 4:6.

31. St. Athanasius, *Discourse Against the Arians,* III, 24.

32. Formally speaking, the Holy Spirit does not share anything with the creature: in this case, it is he who brings about the response of our freedom. The act is completely that of the Holy Spirit and completely our own.

33. Luis M. Martínez, *El Espíritu Santo,* sixth ed. (Madrid, 1959), p. 40.

way by his help, that the ultimate subject, at the basis of our subjectivity, is he."[34]

God does not *order* us to do his will, but he *grants us the gift* of carrying it out and in this way arriving at a flawless interior unity. Thus, the whole of life can be lived day by day under the sign of these words: "Here I am, Lord, to do your will."

Letting Oneself Be Governed by Christ

When God encounters someone who has decided to listen to his voice, he takes that individual's life in his hands and becomes in all reality its *Lord,* its principal vivifying agent. Then to be obedient means fundamentally to be governed by Christ. He holds the rudder of our boat. It is he to whom we present the questions that come up in our lives, certain he will lead us to a happy ending.[35]

Doing the will of God is learned in the same natural manner that, step by step, we learned to walk. Obedience ordinarily is manifested in accepting each day's events, aware that this is where we meet God each moment. It's a beautiful path but not at all easy, for beyond helping us to be calm and content, God wants us to be saints and enjoy his own life to the full. For this reason, after declaring his great love, he wants at once to take from us all confidence in earthly things.

In making Abraham the father of our faith, God uprooted him from family, home, and country. Abraham became a pilgrim who didn't even know where he was going.

---

34. Hans Urs von Balthasar, *El Desconocido más allá del Verbo,* cited in *Comité para el Jubileo del Año 2000, El Espiritu del Señor* (Madrid, 1997), p. 51.
35. See Ex 18:19.

He had only God, whom he followed unconditionally, even when God asked him to sacrifice his son.[36]

What would have happened if Abraham had not been willing to surrender Isaac? If he had rebelled, regarding God's command as too cruel? Perhaps Isaac then might have had to die in battle, or on a journey, or be devoured by wild beasts. No matter the cause of his death—Abraham would have lost him one way or another because he stood between Abraham and God. But in becoming detached from his son, the patriarch not only regained him but at the same time also received the grace of holiness.

At times God deprives us of our safety gear. Other times he invites us to put it aside ourselves, like the widow in the Gospel: "She out of her poverty has put in everything she had, her whole living."[37] She showed an immense trust in God as her all, her sole support.

By contrast, the rich young man lacked that spark of madness that following Christ demands.[38] He wasn't fully alive, restless, and daring. He was a slave of his patrimony and social position, living perhaps for appearances and the certainty of a comfortable life. But making "safety first" your motto can be opposed to excellence. "Stop counting your money and sometimes count the stars instead."[39]

God doesn't want us to act as timid slaves but as his children, filled with confidence and happiness. He wants us to look more at him and less at our surroundings. This is what gives us true independence and great freedom of spirit. Nevertheless, at times we can give in to the temptation to

---

36. See Gen 22:9–13.

37. Mk 12:43–44.

38. See Mk 10:24.

39. Raniero Cantalamessa, *La sobria embriaguez del Espiritu* (*Sober Intoxication of the Spirit*) (Madrid, 1999), p. 164.

betray him by the cowardice of not following what our conscience tells us—for example, out of the fear that no one will
understand what we're doing. Real friends of God don't act
that way. Bl. John Paul II, for instance, once remembered that
some people considered his frequent trips to many parts of
the world excessive. Smiling, he said: "I think these people
are right from a human point of view. But it is God who
is guiding me, and at times he can ask us to do something
per excessum."[40] The voice of conscience comes before any
human judgment, and one day the decisive question will be
whether or not we've been faithful to it.

When, in the midst of our limitations, we see God's power
surrounding and protecting us, we can have freedom of heart
and breathe "with full lungs." There is no need for us to defend
or justify ourselves; we do not depend on human approval.[41]

This doesn't mean we will always understand what
is happening in our life. A Christian will often encounter
perplexing things. God is infinitely greater than we are; his
plans far exceed what we can understand.[42] But they are
full of meaning. God does not guide us by issuing arbitrary
commands, like a Renaissance ruler exalting his caprice
over reason and meaning and flaunting the motto "*stat pro
ratione voluntas*"—"my will is the reason."

Christ demonstrated that it is possible to obey the Father
even in the darkest night: "Not my will, but thine be done."[43]
On the cross, he abandoned himself to God, who seemed to
have abandoned him. He was faithful unto death.

---

40. Bl. John Paul II, cited in Jan Ross, *Der Papst Johannes Paul II. Drama und Geheimnis,* 3rd ed. (Berlin, 2001), p. 129.

41. Ps 118:6: "With the Lord on my side I do not fear. What can man do to me?" See Rom 8:14f.

42. "*Deus semper maior.*" St. Augustine, *Enarratio in Psalmum LXII,* 16.

43. Lk 22:42; see Jn 6:38.

While demanding much, Jesus assured us that his "burden is light."[44] Its lightness is due to the love that gives us wings and lets us fly toward the sky. Do a bird's wings never feel heavy to him? Yes, they do, but without them the bird couldn't rise. They are a light burden for him. "One who is in love," says the *Imitation of Christ*, "flies, runs, and rejoices; he is free, not bound, and nothing can hold him back. Love often knows no limits and overflows all bounds. Love feels no burden, thinks nothing of troubles, attempts more than it is capable of."[45]

Someone united to God lives the unshakeable fascination of being open to the fullness of reality. Everything true, noble, just, pure, and lovable in this world, life and death, present and future—all is his.[46] He feels a great freedom in knowing himself to be a son of God, so loved and submissive that he can apply to himself St. Paul's daring phrase: "All things are lawful for me."[47] All is permissible to him inasmuch as the slightest transgression of the will of his Father is genuinely repugnant to him. Not a slave now, he is a son and a friend, and he can live life as a great feast, a celebration. The French writer Madeleine Delbrêl expresses this in a beautiful poem: [48]

If we were happy with you, O Lord,
we could not resist the need to dance
that permeates the world,
and we would be able to divine

---

44. Mt 11:30.
45. Thomas à Kempis, *The Imitation of Christ*, III, 5.
46. See Phil 4:8; 1 Cor 3:22.
47. 1 Cor 6:12.
48. Madeleine Delbrêl, "Le bal de l'obéissance" in *Nous autres, gens des rues* (Paris: Éditions de Seuil, 1995), p. 81.

what dance it is you would like to have us dance,
following the steps of your Providence.

Because I think that you must be tired
of people who always speak of serving you
with the air of commanders;
of knowing you with the presumption of a professor;
of attaining you through the rules of sport;
of loving you as one loves an old married partner.

To be your good dancing partner
one needn't know where the dance is going.
One has to follow,
to be joyful, to be light,
and above all, not show oneself rigid.
Not to ask why you prefer the steps you choose.

One has to be like an agile, lively extension
of you yourself,
and keep up with the pace of the music as you transmit it.
One mustn't want to go ahead at any cost
but accept taking one's turn
at going sideways,
knowing how to stop and glide rather than walk.

And this would be no more than a series of stupid steps
if the music didn't form a harmony.
But we forget the music of your Spirit
and make of life a gymnastic exercise;
we forget that we are dancing in your arms,
that your holy will is beyond our imagining,
and that the only monotony or boredom
exists among those old souls

who stand motionless in the background
of the joyful dance of your love.

Lord, make us live life
not as a game of chess in which everything is calculated,
not as a match in which everything is difficult,
not as a theorem that puzzles the brain,
but as an endless feast
at which we renew our meeting with you,
as a ball,
as a dance in the arms of your grace,
with the universal music of love.

~6.

OBEYING HUMAN AUTHORITIES: AN EXPRESSION OF FREEDOM

WITH GOOD REASON, THE IMPORTANCE of heeding one's conscience today is emphasized as the key to upright action, harmony with oneself, and following freedom's path. Someone who does not follow his interior light will soon find himself in murky surroundings and then in total darkness, alienated from himself and God.

But given this renewed vision of the dignity and autonomy of each person, can one accept another's commands without demeaning oneself? Can one obey and still remain free? Can one do the will of another and still feel comfortable in one's own "interior home" where no one can enter except God and oneself? These are very timely questions, relevant not only to peaceful and orderly life in society but also to the full realization of each individual.

OBEYING RESPONSIBLY

In the classical and Christian tradition, obedience is considered a virtue. This implies that it can't be exercised without freedom. Goethe places on the lips of Iphigenia a phrase that has become famous: "My soul obeys, and I feel free."[1] Doing another's will without in some way interiorly accepting what one is told to do does not deserve to be called obedience: it is slavishness, hypocrisy, boot licking, or perhaps ambition; in any case, it's the equivalent of a shameful abandonment of personal dignity. Or it may be the appropriate behavior of a dissident who wants to survive in a totalitarian system (as is the case with so-called "internal emigration"); however, then it can't be called obedience but, at best, prudence.

Not Dispensing with Freedom

A person is obedient who does what another wishes *because he also wishes it.* We should never distance ourselves from our interior freedom or from responsibility for our behavior.

Twentieth-century dictatorships taught an important lesson that should never be forgotten: in certain difficult circumstances and under pressure, people are likely to surrender to others decisions about the course a community should adopt and follow. Often they lack the courage to accept responsibility. They prefer not to think, because they know that the least criticism will enormously complicate their lives. And so they come to act as mere instruments, automatons, those who simply carry out what the people in charge decide. They will not refuse to collaborate with even the most horrifying crimes, since they have turned over responsibility for their actions to others; it's "they" who are acting, not themselves.

Consider this exchange between a Nazi functionary and a prosecutor during one of the famous trials after the Second World War.

---

1. Johann Wolfgang von Goethe, *Iphigenia in Tauris*, scene III.

"Did you kill anyone in the concentration camp?"

"Yes."

"Suffocated by gas?"

"Yes."

"Buried alive?"

"That happened sometimes."

"Did you personally help to kill these persons?"

"Not at all, I was only the treasurer of the camp."

"What effects did these actions have on you?"

"It was hard at first, but we became used to it."

"Do you know that the Russians are going to hang you?"

(Breaking into tears): "Why? What did I do?"[2]

Obviously he didn't do anything; he just obeyed orders.

Functionaries of the Nazi state justified their immoral acts by saying they were only obeying orders. Facing loss of employment, exile, the suffering of their families, torture, and death (physical or moral), they shut their ears to their consciences, and some became unscrupulous murderers. Certainly the situation was very complex, and we are not judging individuals here but seeking to understand the human condition: when we count on our own strength only, we are weak and more or less at risk of being externally coerced to do what we shouldn't.

Still, there also are hopeful examples. Moved by the power of the Spirit, the Protestant theologian Dietrich Bonhoeffer, who was cruelly murdered for his resistance to Hitler, wrote while in prison: "I cannot remain quiet, saying my participation is minuscule. Here we do not calculate, and I have to recognize that it is precisely my sin

---

2. See Hannah Arendt, "*La culpabilité organizée*" (1945), in *Penser L'événement* (Paris–Berlin, 1989).

that is guilty of everything."[3] In the same sense, the protagonist in the drama *The Brother of Our God* by Karol Wojtyla speaks of great responsibility "for everything and for everyone."[4]

As a result of experiences like Nazism, people today are highly sensitive regarding this matter of external commands. The generation of 1968 roundly rejected them. They wanted to free themselves from all norms and laws while showing a certain utopian childishness in their rebellion. But the comfortable "alternative culture" of that generation's offspring is even more dangerous. They too are disposed not to obey, but because of laziness rather than ideology. Their parents protested the submissiveness of previous generations, but they cultivate egoistic individualism. Better false ideals than none at all. Better to be wrong than not think.

Obedience today obviously gets bad press. This virtue needs renewal—a middle ground between the mentality that in the Third Reich made possible the murder of millions of innocents in the name of obeying orders, and the mentality that gave rise to the student revolutions and later to an utter blindness toward values. How can a Christian of the third millennium live and cultivate obedience with dignity and humility?

The virtue of obedience presupposes the personal consciousness of being interiorly independent of men and united to God. At the same time, it inclines one voluntarily to do as the other wishes, provided always that it is consistent with one's own light; otherwise, it leads one to protest courageously against what tramples on human dignity. It was in this sense that Bl. John Paul II said the Christian

---

3. Dietrich Bonhoeffer, *Éthique* (Geneva, 1965).
4. See Karol Wojtyla (Bl. John Paul II), *The Brother of Our God.*

future of a country "depends on how many people are sufficiently mature to be nonconformists."[5]

We can never abandon the freedom purchased by our Savior's blood. Only on that condition can we obey.

Knowing What You Are Doing

Obedience without freedom is a contradiction, a "squaring of the circle." It is going through the motions, without enthusiasm, without love or understanding, and unworthy of a human being. Someone who acts according to rules he doesn't accept interiorly or whose meaning he doesn't understand is not free. He acts in a subhuman manner or, in the case of the dissident, in the manner of a prisoner.

Since obedience is closely related to freedom, both the intellect and the will are involved in its exercise. Intelligent obedience means, above all, that I understand not only the command but also its significance—its connection with a goal worthy of being attained. If, for example, I must spend all day in a factory operating a transmission belt that carries a certain metal part, but I don't know whether it's a part in an auto or a tank, I'm not free. I don't understand my role in the larger scheme. And if the people in charge don't explain it to me, if they withhold information or manipulate it, they're treating me as a small child or a robot, not as an adult who can decide things for himself.

For an action to be considered one's own, a person must know what he or she wants to accomplish by it. One isn't free if one is directed in one's work from an external source that doesn't communicate the work's meaning (or may even misrepresent it). Someone in this situation is like a blind-

---

5. Bl. John Paul II, cited in Jan Ross, *Der Papst Johannes Paul II: Drama und Geheimnis*, 3rd ed. (Berlin, 2001), p. 93.

folded man being led by another. The guide shouldn't just praise the beauty of the path he's treading but remove the blindfold and allow him to see for himself.

Blind obedience produces blind men, people who perhaps collaborate in building an atomic bomb or cloning human beings *without knowing it.* Throughout history this attitude of exaggerated dependence on authority, divorced from autonomous thinking and without a shred of critical sense, has led more than a few people to participate in inflicting day-in and day-out suffering on others. For instance, some teachers, wedded to archaic ideas about pedagogy, have forbidden their students to play with a child who was a bit unruly or with a little gypsy, in order to keep them from associating with a supposed "bad apple." How many parents protested this lack of humanity? How many tried to understand the child who was "difficult" and increasingly sad as a result of being isolated? "If you want someone to be good, treat him as if he were good already." The truth of this bit of popular wisdom speaks for itself, while the ancient wisdom of the Christian tradition rightly counsels us to ask God's pardon for our own unknown sins.

According to St. Thomas, "The greatness of a virtue should not be measured from the point of view of its difficulty, but taking into account its intrinsic goodness."[6] I do good when I act in conformity with the truth, not necessarily when I obey. I do evil when I don't act in conformity with truth and not always when I don't obey. Obedience is not an end in itself; it is a means that helps bring me closer to the end. The positive element—doing God's will—is more important than the negative—not doing one's own original will.

---

6. Aquinas, *Summa Theologiae* II-II, q. 123, a. 12 c.; q. 115, a. 4 c.

The best kind of obedience is not blind (which doesn't even merit being called obedience) but that which sees clearly. It leads us to see through the eyes of another, inasmuch as we have identified—perhaps after a great struggle—with his will. Then our outlook is broadened, and we can say with conviction: "I want what you want."

Trusting in Others

Our conscience is more important than all external precepts. Cardinal Newman expressed this in a well-known letter to the Duke of Norfolk. "If I am obliged to bring religion into after-dinner toasts (which indeed does not seem quite the thing), I shall drink—to the Pope, if you please—still to Conscience first, and to the Pope afterwards."[7] Every man has to follow the truth he himself has found. (For this, in the first place, he toasts conscience.) On the other hand, man is obliged by his very nature to seek the full truth, to form himself well, and to seek help from someone else with more light. (Thus, we understand why Newman next toasts the Pope.)

We do not always understand all the advice others give us, but at least we can understand that we have limitations and that four eyes see more than two. That someone else's perspective is different from mine can enrich me enormously as a source of more data, new arguments, and better solutions to problems.

If the other not only advises but commands, exercising legitimate authority over me, and I don't understand his will, I still can obey provided two indispensable conditions are met. We've already seen the first and most fundamental of these: that my conscience not tell me anything to the contrary.

---

7. J.H. Newman, *Carta al Duque de Norfolk* (*Letter to the Duke of Norfolk*) 2nd ed. (Rialp, 2005), p. 82.

Second, it is necessary that we trust the authority of the other. If he or she is an honest person who has shown us interest and affection and who sincerely seeks the good of all, it's not difficult to obey, even if "I don't see the point." Even when I have reasons for seriously doubting this person's grasp of the situation or even his or her virtue, I can follow the commands on the basis of prudence provided I'm confident that God means to communicate his will through this person (this ordinarily occurs among Christians in spiritual direction or in counseling). In this case, aware of my own limitations and how easily I go astray, I make an act of supernatural faith: rather than obeying this particular person, I obey God himself, speaking to me through him or her. I am not trusting in a human being's excellence but in God's goodness. Yet if I cannot make this free act of faith and trust, neither can I obey.[8]

Let's return to the sphere of human relations. There are in fact circumstances that make obedience difficult. For example, when someone lies to us and deceives us, not considering us worthy of the truth, we find it hard to consider that person deserving of our trust. Observing that someone sees us as a hindrance or a danger, we spontaneously close up in his or her presence, sensing that this person might do us injury. In these circumstances, it can be very hard—and even inadvisable—to do what the other person wants: one naturally prefers self-defense to self-destruction.

It's impossible to follow someone you don't trust, someone who expresses indifference or contempt for people. This was the situation in Germany, at least at the beginning of

---

8. "In those things that concern the interior movement of the will, no one is obliged to obey another person, but only God." Aquinas, *Summa Theologiae* II–II, q. 94, a. 5 c.

the Nazi regime. When Hitler and his party came to power, ordinary citizens couldn't clearly see the evil that was at hand, but they surely knew they now were facing a world of lies. Thus Hitler had many slaves who were compelled to be such, along with a few obedient subjects, who identified with his corrupt will and soon rose to be rulers themselves.

Often someone doesn't grasp the full extent of a command. But at least he needs to grasp its basic meaning or else obedience could have absurd results. For instance, in some countries like Spain, it's fashionable for young people to engage in *"la movida"* on weekends—at midnight visiting bars and clubs with friends and coming home drunk at seven the next morning. A mother once explained to some fifteen-year-old boys that barhopping at night wasn't a good idea. The boys wanted to obey. So they stopped going to bars and instead gathered at somebody's house at midnight, and *then* came home drunk at seven in the morning. They didn't understand what they'd been told, so their obedience was a caricature.

GOVERNING WITH PRUDENCE

Every crisis of obedience is preceded by a crisis of authentic authority. In the sixteenth century, the Protestant reformer Calvin succeeded in enforcing God's law with extreme rigor in the city of Geneva. He organized not only public life, but also the private lives of citizens, determining in even the smallest details what they should do or avoid doing every day to give God maximum glory. Games, dances, and shows were prohibited. Everything was under the control of the authorities, with a complex system of espionage and denunciation in place. The members of the government had the right to drop in unannounced on any family at any time to make sure the family members were doing as they should. A hairdresser who made a striking coiffure for a woman is said to have been punished with two days in prison. And so the city's face was completely changed. The joy of living gave way to strict repression. Soon, though, the people's liberal spirit led them to reject the system and organize a fierce resistance to the reformer.[9]

Appropriate Legislation

Someone who wants to be obeyed should issue few commands. In forming people at all levels, it's best to insist on some clear, essential points, and then allow great spontaneity and freedom that make allowances for each one's particular mentality, character, and situation. When there are rules even for the minutiae of everyday life, the result will be to produce personalities that are stunted, oppressed, and stifled by this tightly knit regulatory network. Passivity and sadness will be the result. Human beings not only *are* free but need to *feel* free in order to act with creativity and joy.

In some totalitarian systems, the authorities post so many roadside prohibitions that travelers are in danger of losing their way and missing the natural beauty around them. Instead they travel in constant fear, holding their breath, as if constantly at risk of having an accident. It seems better not to leave one's comfortable and secure home in order to see the world and experience something new. Some day those lawmakers may be called to give more of an account for the good they prevented than for the evil they prevented.

This problem has always existed. In Jesus' day the people were oppressed by the arid, interminable decrees of

---

9. See Jutta Burggraf, *Conocerse y comprenderse. Una introducción al ecumenismo,* 2nd ed. (Madrid, 2003), pp. 184–191.

the law, invoked by the priests, Pharisees, and scribes.[10] In this environment, the words of the Son of God rang out as something completely new, causing many to raise their heads and begin to feel that longed-for freedom in which they no longer believed: "Happy because you are loved, happy the weaker you are, the smaller, the poorer, happy because I know your sufferings, happy because I will remedy them."[11] Jesus did not tax people with a lot of rules and observances, which encumber fervent hearts and create bureaucrats of the spiritual life. In his presence, everyone felt accepted, understood, and protected.[12] They could lay down their burdens, rest, and recover the joy of living.[13]

Neither Forcing nor Manipulating Others

That each person is the image of God, especially in his interior freedom, is more clearly understood now than in earlier times. Under no pretext may we destroy this image. And that is what someone does in trying to prevent another from living according to his deepest convictions.[14] So long as those convictions do not impinge upon the rights of others, it is better that one be allowed to act according to one's conscience, even in something that is, perhaps, objectively evil, than to force one to do good under coercion.[15]

---

10. See Acts 15:10: "Why do you make trial of God by putting a yoke upon the neck of the disciples which neither our fathers nor we have been able to bear?"

11. See Lk 11:37–54.

12. See Mt 9:10f; Lk 7:37f.

13. See Mt 11:28.

14. *Dignitatis Humanae* (*DH*), 12: "Although in the life of the people of God in its pilgrimage through the vicissitudes of human history there has at times appeared a form of behavior which was hardly in keeping with the spirit of the Gospel and was even opposed to it, it has always remained the teaching of the Church that no one is to be coerced into believing." See *Dignitatis Humanae,* 3.

15. See Rocco Buttiglione, "*Zur Philosophie von Karol Wojtyla,*" in *Johannes Paul II. Zeuge des Evangeliums,* ed. by St. Horn SDS (Wurzburg: A. Riebel, 1999), pp. 36–39.

This attitude of profound respect was shown, for example, by the last Polish king of the Jagiellonian dynasty. At a time when the trials of the Inquisition were taking place and heretics were being burned at the stake in the West, he demonstrated his prudence in assuring his subjects, "I am not the king of your consciences."[16]

At the end of the seventeenth century in France, nonetheless, preachers admonished people to obey all royal precepts, no matter how capricious. But as eager as they were to preach obedience to the people, these same preachers were much less concerned to remind the sovereign of his obligations to his people. Bishop Fenelon, "a drop of authenticity in a sea of falsehood," dared to call the attention of the Sun King to the limits of his authority and was expelled from the palace as punishment for his presumption.[17]

There is no denying that Christians in some periods pressured and manipulated those who thought differently, even persecuting and punishing them, as was the custom in those times. Starting often from the principle that "error has no rights," they interpreted it to mean that the *persons* they considered in error had no case to make—though no doubt they often acted with good intentions, and it would be unfair to judge yesterday's events by today's ways of thinking.

We should learn from history. Violence, torture, and terror aren't licit ways of getting someone to do good. "For Christ . . . meek and humble of heart, acted patiently in attracting and inviting his disciples. . . . [he] refused to use force."[18] One *cannot* force anyone to be good. The Church

---

16. Bl. John Paul II, *Cruzando el umbral de la Esperanza* (*Crossing the Threshold of Hope*) (Barcelona, 1994), p. 160.

17. François Fénelon (1641–1715), was a teacher of the princes in the court of Louis XIV.

18. *Dignitatis Humanae*, 11. The text makes reference to Mt 9:28f; Mt 11:28–30; Mk 9:23f.; Jn 5:67–78.

has wisely condemned "any action which seems to suggest coercion or dishonest or unworthy persuasion especially when dealing with the uneducated or the poor."[19] And it has declared firmly: "Truth can impose itself on the mind of man only in virtue of its own truth, which wins over the mind with both gentleness and power." [20]

Spiritual Guidance: Helping Others to Mature

Conscience is the most sacred aspect of the person; it is the place where God speaks and where each person decides his or her own destiny.[21] One who exercises authority over others has a grave duty to bear this in mind. He must show a profound respect for others. Each human being is a singular jewel to be polished, not broken or cut in order to become just like the others.

Unfortunately, some people don't seem to know what to do with their freedom. This is especially true because they don't know how to listen to God's voice within them. When confronted with the need to make a decision, to choose one path or another, they become anxious and fearful, afraid lest they make a mistake, afraid to commit themselves, to realize their dreams, afraid of sinning and being punished. They look for someone to relieve them of their anxious burdens, perhaps even someone to counsel their consciences. But they forget that real help involves much more than just giving pious advice. They actually don't want someone to help them gradually become self-directing—just the oppo-

---

19. *DH* 4.

20. *DH* 1. See Bl. John Paul II, encyclical *Ut Unum Sint*, 3. Bl. John Paul II did not hesitate to affirm that the Church *laments* having used "intolerant methods and even violence in the service of the truth" which obscured more than a little the light of Christ. Idem, Apostolic Letter *Tertio Millennio Adveniente*, 35.

21. See *Gaudium et Spes*, 14.

site: they want to be freed from themselves, to hand over responsibility to someone else. This is why it's easy for them to accept direction. While seeming to be very obedient, self-denying, and virtuous, they remain adolescents, forever children, in the interior life.

A good spiritual counselor will understand this situation and, looking deeper, will uncover the lack of a well-formed personality, the childishness lying behind a façade of adaptation to family and social norms. More important than submission in these circumstances are bonds of mutual confidence that can lead the immature person to engage in self-examination, consider and accept his own complexes and fears, and finally overcome them with another's help.

The most important task of a spiritual guide is to show the other person how to use his freedom, which is not an oppressive burden but a gift of God meant to make him happy. One who only gives orders and demands that they be carried out without teaching the immature person to listen to God's voice in his heart is not a help but a threat, a facilitator of the other person's childishness.[22] "Spiritual guidance should not be used to turn people into beings with no judgment of their own, who limit themselves to carrying out mechanically what others tell them. On the contrary, it should tend to develop men and women with their own Christian standards."[23]

---

22. See Gerhard L. Müller, *Mit der Kirche denken* (Würzburg, 2001), pp. 131ff.

23. St. Josemaría Escrivá, *Conversations*, no. 93. Idem., no. 29: "It is a matter of making each person aware of his own responsibilities and of inviting him to accept them according to the dictates of his conscience, acting with full freedom." Idem. No. 104: "Advice does not take away freedom. It gives elements on which to judge and thus enlarges the possibilities of choice and ensures that decisions are not taken on the basis of irrational factors. After hearing the opinions of others and taking everything into consideration, there comes a moment in which a choice has to be made and then no one has the right to force a person's freedom."

To develop or form others means to free within them their God-given powers and help them achieve their full natural and supernatural development.

OBEYING GOD RATHER THAN MEN:
THE PRIORITY OF GOD'S WILL

In carrying out human commands, an adult person has both the right and the *obligation* to consult his or her conscience. "We must obey God rather than men." With this famous affirmation before the Sanhedrin, applicable in all epochs, St. Peter proclaimed freedom of conscience as a general principle.[24] Not even the supreme lawgiver of a state can order whatever he pleases. Above his authority there is a higher power, that of God, whom human lawgivers also must obey.

Sophocles focused this problem in *Antigone*. The heroine of this classic tragedy disobeyed the orders of the king in order to follow the voice of her conscience. She buried the body of her beloved brother, thereby incurring the penalty of capital punishment. In one scene, her lover Haemon confronted his father Creon, the king, saying, "I am your son and I follow you, when you govern with wisdom."[25]

A person who disobeys unjust human laws can be profoundly *obedient*, while someone else who obeys is in reality *disobedient*. No one can hide behind obedience to man and doing what is "politically correct" in order to refuse obedience to God. So, for instance, no doctor has a right to perform an abortion or euthanasia even if the civil law requires it.

---

24. Acts 5:29.
25. Sophocles, *Antigone*, episode 3.

Thomas Aquinas pointed out that the mature citizen, while showing himself affable with simple people, is "great" with the powerful, and he avoids lowering himself by adulation or dissimulation.[26] "The law should be obeyed with the soul of a king."[27] St. Thomas himself was severely criticized by his contemporaries for taking seriously the pagan philosophy of Aristotle and integrating it into his own thought. Fortunately, he did not pay attention to those who wanted to put obstacles in his way. Moved by an interior strength, he succeeded in achieving an admirable synthesis between reason and faith.

And yet a Christian isn't a revolutionary. While setting God's will above the power of men, he displays profound respect for all legitimate authority.

Epikeia: The Importance of a "Prudent Flexibility"

Epikeia (equity) is an ancient virtue related to prudence. It refers to interpreting law according to the spirit of the legislator, and not according to the "dead letter."[28] It follows from the principle enunciated by St. Peter, that we should obey God before men. "In Christ a new will of God has been manifested, which is the fulfillment of all the preceding ones; to continue obeying the old order would mean to disobey. . . . Obedience to the truth is obedience to the new, obedience to the *New* Testament."[29] It is obedience to the Spirit that brings to life and makes us understand the true meaning of the law.

---

26. See Aquinas *Summa Theologiae* II–II, q. 120, a.3, ad 5.

27. August Adam, *La virtud de la libertad* (Orig. *Die Tugend der Freiheit*) (San Sebastián, 1957) p. 164.

28. See 2 Cor 3:6 "The written code kills, but the Spirit gives life." Aquinas *Summa Theologiae* II-II, q. 120 a. 1 c.: *Epikeia* is a virtue that "setting aside the letter of the law, follows the dictates of justice and the common good."

29. Cantalamessa, *Obediencia*, 3rd ed. (Valencia 2002), p. 33.

In Christ's day, the mechanical and exterior fulfillment of the law had become the main thing: the intimate delicacy of conscience was a secondary matter. "You tithe mint and dill and cumin, and have neglected the weightier matters of the Law, justice and mercy and faith."[30] The Pharisees kept people trapped in constant quandaries of conscience.[31] An honorable Israelite became first a slave of the Law's text, and then a slave of its interpreters.

For example, the Jews who condemned the Son of God "did not enter the praetorium, so that they might not be defiled, but might eat the Passover."[32] They could unite their blind hatred to meticulous observance of external rites handed down from earlier generations. The letter of the law meant more to them than justice. And their self-assurance in acting showed that group solidarity (important though it was) prevented them from seeing their own faults.[33]

St. Paul took up his fight against mere external fulfillment of the commandments with that ardor and enthusiasm that had welled up in his heart ever since that day outside Damascus. His letters testify clearly to it.[34] Here was a stiff battle between narrowness and broadness of principles—generous freedom and meticulous literal interpretation of a host of inherited norms that tended to exalt a kind of ascetical gymnastics. "But now we are discharged from the law, dead to that which held us captive, so that we serve not under the old written code but in the new life of the Spirit."[35]

---

30. Mt 23:23.
31. See Mt 23:4.
32. See Jn 18:28.
33. See Mt 23:25.
34. See Gal 5:1: "Stand fast therefore, and do not submit again to a yoke of slavery." Eph 6:5 and Col 3:23: A Christian has to obey "by his conscience," "in singleness of heart."
35. Rom 7:6.

This doesn't mean the commandments are superfluous. Since sin entered human life, they constitute an indispensable help in distinguishing true movements of the Spirit from false ones and directing our actions toward the good. But the conduct of the Christian is inspired, first of all, not by the dry words of the law but by the ardent charity inflaming and enlivening all that he does. What matters, in the long run, is not that something be difficult or costly, but that it be true. Love and mercy are more likely to accompany truth than exaggerated rigor.

Epikeia does not weaken the force of the law. On the contrary, someone who makes use of it wishes to carry out the legislator's will.[36] Sometimes one will feel moved not to do the specific act prescribed by the text of the law; other times one may feel obliged to do a good work that no law requires—for example, give up certain rights and advantages even though the law allows them. A rich man can't seize all of a poor man's possessions and plunge him into misery, even though a legal code might give him that right. "*Summum ius, summa iniuria*": the maximum "justice" can lead someone to do the worst injury if consideration is not given to the special circumstances of a particular situation.[37] Thus a person can be authorized—and even obliged—to diverge from the letter of the law, appealing to what he seriously believes is its true spirit.

All the same, *epikeia* clearly can't be considered either the rallying cry of rebels or a final solution for rare, isolated cases. It is part of the authentic ethics and basic values of Christian morality. Some fear to acknowledge each Chris-

---

36. See Aquinas, *Summa Theologiae* II–II, q. 120 a. 1 ad 1: *Epikeia* is not "opposed to severity, which follows the letter of the law when it ought to be followed."

37. Bl. John Paul II includes this famous sentence in his encyclical *Dives in Misericordia*, 12.

tian's right to decide independently of the written law, but that simply underlines the urgent need to give solid formation to all. *Epikeia* isn't an exception; it's a normal function for every mature Christian.

Commands shouldn't be rigid principles that stifle our aspirations and desires, along with our true interest in others' needs and in solidarity. Jesus relativized the "old" Law, subordinating it to profound attitudes of the heart and the needs of one's neighbor in which reside the fulfillment of the "new" law of love.

He taught us that we should not freeze and paralyze tradition, locking it forever in the past. Traditions need to be reinterpreted according to the demands presented by each new situation. A Christian needs to find God in his own time and place.[38] "In the whole history of the world there is one single important hour, which is the present. Whoever flees from the present is fleeing from the hour of God."[39]

A biography of St. Ignatius Loyola recounts an incident in which a Jesuit superior insisted that an order from the founder of the Society of Jesus be carried out according to the letter, without taking circumstances into account. St. Ignatius sharply reproached him and canceled his order, saying: "But could it be that I, when I gave that order, by chance, took away from you the spirit of charity and prudent discretion?"[40] *Epikeia* is more perfect than literal obe-

---

38. See Acts 17:26.

39. Dietrich Bonhoeffer, *Predigten, Auslegungen, Meditationen* I (1984), p. 196f.

40. Daniello Bartoli, *Biografia de San Ignacio* (*History of the Life and Institute of St. Ignatius Loyola*) III, p. 44, cited in A. Adam, *La virtud de la libertad*, cit., p. 308f.

41. Aquinas, *Summa Theologiae* II-II, q. 120 a. 2 ad 2. See ibid. q. 120 a. 2c: "*Epikeia* is a rule superior to human acts." Ibid., q. 120, a. 2, ad 1: "*Epikeia* is the principal part of legal justice."

dience and in a certain sense is justice itself.[41] It puts down roots in the most intimate part of the human heart, where one is alone with God and feels accountable to him—and only him—regarding the reasons for one's decisions. One who takes *epikeia* seriously realizes his or her immense responsibility. But such a person can be confident that he is never alone. The divine Spirit moves us to interpret correctly the laws that regulate our lives. If we are disposed to listen to his voice—not only within us but also speaking through the legitimate authority that transmits his wishes to us—we can become obedient and free, strong and flexible, like those great trees so spectacularly shaken by the winds of storms and hurricanes, yet without breaking because their roots go very deep.

Being Strong and Humble

Although everyone enjoys an enormous dignity, we've all been born with old, hard hearts, wounded by sin and full of egoistic desires. Thus, at times we tend to look with jaundiced eyes at the Church, our Mother, and its representatives as if they were enemies of our happiness and obstacles to our complete self-fulfillment when with their mandates they close off the rocky roads that lead to corruption. The greater the sin, the greater our unheeding resentment of human authorities and, in the end, of God, even to the point of wishing he didn't exist.

The coming of the Holy Spirit works a miracle, transforming our stony hearts into hearts of flesh: vulnerable, compassionate, and open.[42] Beginning to see the world from a renewed perspective, we discover that God and his repre-

---

42. See Ezekiel 36:26–27.

sentatives aren't our adversaries but the allies of our well-being. From then on, it's no longer difficult to have trust: we can consider their counsels and commands as being in the service of the interior voice of the Spirit that in its turn moves us to obey from within.[43]

Human law, if it is just, also manifests God's will to us. Understanding it as an active commitment, made in the interior of the heart, we can perhaps convert it into a principle of life for ourselves. The mature exercise of freedom doesn't consist in just doing as I feel but doing what is right and carrying out my life's project—that is to say, God's will for me.

Where the Holy Spirit acts, free and responsible obedience results. His presence evokes the desire to follow the commands we have received and, as much as possible, do what others ask of us. We are "servants of Christ, doing the will of God from the heart."[44]

St. Basil distinguished three dispositions with which one can obey: through fear of punishment—the disposition of slaves; from a desire for a reward— the disposition of mercenaries; for love—the disposition of children.[45] Love is the true source of Christian obedience. It shows us the fruitfulness of the law and makes us capable of accepting even the hardest sacrifices with a smile. Solid and upright virtue is marked by a shining interior joy and a natural inclination toward the good.

---

43. See St. John Chrysostom, *Homily on the Gospel of Matthew*, I: "The apostles did not descend from the mountain like Moses, bearing in their hands tablets of stone. They came out of the cenacle carrying the Spirit in their hearts . . . as if they were books animated by the grace of the Holy Spirit."

44. Eph 6:6.

45. See St. Basil. *Reg. fus. Proem*: PL 31, 896; in Cantalamessa, *Obedience*, cit., p. 17.

The ideal of obedience doesn't mean giving up one's intellect, but rather collaborating conscientiously in the great work of the Kingdom of God with great faithfulness and enthusiasm under the direction of legitimate authorities.

Nevertheless, it is good to bear in mind that in one way or another, personal weakness, pride, and laziness will be with us all our days. Even after many years of struggle, it can be hard to follow another's will. In these circumstances it is good to look to Christ, who, "obedient even unto death," gave himself for us to free us more and more from the weight of our sins, opening our hearts wide to his liberating grace and patiently forming us in the art of living healthy lives.

Where the Holy Spirit is active, there is neither rigidity nor childishness but mature love. One who is truly free, living with God, respects the consciences of others. Understanding those who can't help interpreting the law in a scrupulous manner, he tries not to give them any cause to be scandalized. "If food is a cause of my brother's falling, I will never eat meat, lest I cause my brother to fall," said St. Paul, the great champion of Christian freedom.[46] There is no merit in lacking a knack for flexibility and being so focused on abstract truths that one fails to see the real world consequences of one's actions.

In his homily on the canonization of Teresa Benedicta of the Cross (Edith Stein), Bl. John Paul II proposed as a model for us this holy martyr who says to all: "Do not accept anything as the truth if it lacks love. And do not accept anything as love that lacks truth! One without the

---

46. 1 Cor 8:13. See Rom 14:21: "It is right not to eat meat or drink wine or do anything that makes your brother stumble."

other becomes a destructive lie."[47] Every truth mixed with poison becomes false.

To the extent that divine grace makes us humble and obedient, we will be able to praise God with all our hearts, all our ability, with intellect, will, and the rich world of our feelings, with memory and imagination, and even with our most hidden thoughts and desires.

---

47. Bl. John Paul II, *Homily at the Canonization of St. Teresa Benedicta of the Cross, Edith Stein,* October 11, 1998.

❧7.

OBSTACLES IN THE ROAD

THOUGH WE HAVE NEVER HAD SUCH an acute and well-developed sense of freedom as we do now, it hasn't been able to prevent the emergence of "new forms of social and psychic slavery"[1] in societies so extensively ruled by the means of communication.

EXTERNAL PRESSURES

Chains of gold bind large sectors of today's globalized world. There is a tyranny of the masses and of social conventions. It is not difficult to see a powerful collectivist current at work, operating to rob us of the most private part of our selves for the sake of egalitarianism and uniformity—if not among everyone, then at least among those linked to particular parties, associations, communities, Web pages, or golf clubs. It's stylish to sing the same song, dress alike, and use the same prefabricated arguments expressed with the same words, the same looks, and even the same smiles. A woman who had lived for several decades in Africa that

---

1. *Gaudium et Spes*, 4.

returned recently to Spain was surprised in the airport to see "waves of yellow and blue." That summer, all the women had yellow and blue dresses, slacks, skirts, blouses, jackets, raincoats, hats, shoes, bags, necklaces, bracelets, and earrings.

Many people don't notice their chains. They readily adapt themselves to the general spirit as they encounter it. Their feelings, thoughts, and words aren't their own; they are premade feelings, thoughts, and phrases spread abroad in thousands of newspapers and magazines, on the radio, television, and the Internet. Romano Guardini spoke of the "phenomenon of automatism" as characterizing not just the world of technology, but our whole way of living.[2] Once people begin to think and act on their own and hold opinions different from those generally accepted by the system—closed in on itself and refusing to recognize anything it might find bothersome—they are simply rejected.

We cannot deny that the world can indeed be a difficult place. For example, in not a few Western societies that think of themselves as free there is real, overt interference in the exercise of personal rights. Conscientious objection to unjust laws is not tolerated. A mayor who refuses to solemnize a "marriage" between homosexual persons must be prepared to be *persona non grata* from that moment on: ridiculed, admonished, and in some European countries even dismissed from his post. And this is just one example among many.

Now and then it's useful to recall the famous novel *1984*. Decades ago, George Orwell gave a graphic account of the horror of a possible future world order based on lies and psychological violence, "a world of fear and treachery,

---

2. See Romano Guardini, "*Askese als Element der menschlichen Existenz,*" in Guardini and Eduard Spranger, *Vom stilleren Leben* (Würzburg, 1956), p. 40.

a world of trampling and being trampled upon, a world which will grow not less but more merciless as it refines itself. . . . If you want a picture of the future, imagine a boot stomping on a human face—forever." The people in this story are controlled by fear of the all-powerful figure of Big Brother. The protagonist is persecuted and mentally tortured until he loses all creativity and the power to rebel. At the end, it is clear that the personality of even the most courageous can be crushed by depriving him of his fundamental right to freedom.[3]

SLAVERY TO SIN

How can the evil that surrounds you affect you? It has the power to change and even destroy your exterior life, but it can only do real damage to the extent that it finds some complicity within you, inasmuch as you identify with it interiorly.

A Christian who is conscious that God himself is supporting him from the most profound depths of his heart has the strength to live calmly in the midst of turmoil. At times, though, we forget this presence of God and let ourselves be dominated by hastiness, lack of tranquility, or anxiety. It's as if we set Jesus aside, emerge alone from our "dwelling place," and say to him, "I can't count on you now. I need to take charge of this matter personally." A time of misfortune often reveals how much faith and confidence we still lack.

Dependence on Man

We are invited to develop our interiority and live serenely under the affectionate gaze of our Father God, in the com-

---

3. See George Orwell, *1984* (London and New York, 1949), p. 230.

pany of Jesus himself, who wants always to encourage, strengthen, and console us. Unfortunately, though, we frequently reject this beautiful option and overlook the beauty of our destiny. We live in the external world as if it were the most important one, the only one, seeking success and material well-being at any cost and ever more compulsively. If you believe the most important thing is to have the most expensive car that suits your image as a powerful executive, you are entirely at the mercy of what others think. Enjoying life is thus impossible. We lose ourselves in thousands of trivialities and block the rhythm of our inner nature. The accumulation of goods reveals itself to be a high-risk enterprise, a source not of joy but sorrow, an object of derision.[4] As St. John of the Cross says, it matters little whether a bird is tied with a thick cord or a silken thread. The result is the same: the bird can't fly![5]

At certain moments we may be more affected by what other people think of us than what God thinks. Then we decide to live apart from the loving presence of Christ, before the critical eyes of men whose judgments can only be limited and incomplete and are often unjust, even cruel. This is the beginning of endless conflicts where we see the essence and tragedy of sin: not desiring friendship with God, we end up depending on men.

Sin lies at the root of a lack of freedom. It gives just the opposite of what it promises—slavery instead of freedom.[6] It forces us to live in the world as slaves: *living to pretend*— acting to obtain some passing approval bestowed ultimately by caprice. The truth of this is easily seen: How often have

---

4. See Mt 19:16–22; Lk 12:16–21.
5. See St. John of the Cross, *The Ascent of Mt. Carmel* 1, 11, 4.
6. See Jn 8:34; Rom 6:16–17.

we felt ourselves pressured to do something that we basically hate merely to get some trivial good?[7] St. Paul gets to the heart of it: "The wages of sin is death"[8]—the death of freedom as well.

How can you be interiorly free in a society that measures you by what you produce? Many people complain that they can't live as they would like. But if we look a little deeper, we see that these people have absorbed the expectations of society. They want to be free, but they also want to get ahead and receive official recognition. They are constantly changing their colors to earn men's esteem and win further advancement. This way of acting robs them of dignity and deforms them. "The saddest thing is to encounter people who have obtained a deserved prestige in their professional lives, who have become competent doctors, great artisans, researchers, or artists and who, nevertheless, in the autumn of life—which should be a natural time of serenity and quiet—feel themselves unfortunate, unsuccessful, and lonely."[9]

Many people suffer because others decide for them. They haven't been able to build up confidence in themselves, because others have taken it away—a coworker who criticizes them constantly, a bad-tempered neighbor, an unhappy cousin. We give others power over us by making ourselves dependent on their moods. Some people's state of mind depends entirely on those they live with. If someone chides them, they feel desolate. If someone else comes home with a long face, they become sad or feel guilty. They let others decide who they are, and they even start to consider themselves good or bad according to how others regard

---

7. See Rom 7:14ff.
8. Rom 6:23.
9. Jose Morales Marín, "Virgo Veneranda," in *Scripta de Maria* VIII (1985), p. 433.

them. Without protest or reason, they submit to the implacable rule of their accusers.

False feelings of guilt can arise not from what is evil in God's eyes, but what is bad in the eyes of society and its conventions. How easily we forget the words of David in the *Miserere*: "Against thee, thee only, have I sinned, and done that which is evil in thy sight." It is beneath a man's dignity to make himself another's slave. We should never degrade ourselves like that and abdicate our own judgment.

Loss of Interior Harmony

Sin makes men into slaves, but prisoners of themselves first of all. It is a destructive power that rules despotically.[10] It shatters interior harmony, producing darkness in the intellect, weakness in the will, and disorder in the affections. Thus, as we distance ourselves from God, we become distanced and alienated from ourselves. In time, we are no longer our own, since we are unable to live at ease in this dirty, ruined house of ours in which evil has installed itself like an occupying force in wartime.[11]

In this situation, one can engage in evasive tactics by pursuing "activity for activity's sake." Some people are forever too busy, always looking for things to do, rushing for no good reason, unable to listen to anyone, arranging their affairs so as never to be alone for a minute. Behind that hyperactivity may lie wounded pride, deception, and above all the compulsion to prove something to oneself and others, to flee something, to avoid thinking or facing up to real problems.

Sin is self-negation. The Hong Kong film producer Wong Kar-Wai expressed this in an extraordinary way in the movie

---

10. See Rom 5:12 and 8:2, 20–21.
11. See Rom 7:14: man is "sold to sin."

In the Mood for Love.[12] The faces of an unfaithful couple never appear on the screen. The audience sees their bodily forms, hears them speaking on the phone, but can't see their features. It's as if infidelity destroyed their identity. By contrast, a faithful couple are presented as wonderfully valuable and attractive, fully themselves, real people with unmistakable faces—and a great capacity to struggle and live.

Sin leads us into the tunnel of dissatisfaction, creating a kind of general discomfort. One no longer feels at home in one's own skin. But someone who doesn't care to be with himself will not enjoy being anywhere. And in seeking to better one's situation, one may become more and more egocentric.

When we focus upon ourselves and our whims, we are not free, nor do we have strength to give ourselves to others. St. Augustine provided a simple example. A husband with a lot of love gave a precious ring to his wife. But she liked the ring more than her husband, and once it was on her finger, she took no notice of his presence. For her, the ring, a sign of love, had become a threat that separated her from the one who loved her and led her to ruin.[13] Something similar occurs when the world, instead of being a path to knowing God and elevating us toward him, begins to be everything for us, an enclosed, self-sufficient reality that points to nothing beyond itself. Then we become entrapped by stunted options—myopic, utilitarian, or simply consumerist—while the pure water of the interior channel stagnates, becoming a fetid pool filled with strange creatures.[14]

---

12. Released in 1999.

13. St. Augustine, *On the First Letter of St. John*, 2, 11: PL 35, 1995.

14. See St. Augustine, *The Happy Life*, 2:10: "Lo and behold, everyone . . . says that those who live as they please are happy. That is a big mistake! Because to desire what is not good is the summit of misfortune. It is not so much not to attain what you desire as it is to obtain what is not good for you, because perversity of the will brings greater evils than fortune brings good": PL 32, 964.

A TWISTED PERSONALITY

In Communist countries years ago, someone considered "normal" for having learned to fit in was often less sane than someone who landed in a psychiatric hospital, having been pronounced "neurotic" by the authorities. The patient was simply being authentic, while the one who enjoyed prestige and health had been despoiled of his individuality and spontaneity, assuming an artificial identity composed purely of appearances.

Something similar happens in our societies. With effort, we construct fictitious identities for ourselves so as to be "just like everyone else." We lack the courage to be different because we fear that then no one would accept us. But a false identity is a very fragile thing, since it is founded upon an immense interior vacuum. Sustaining it requires a great expenditure of energy, and when we can no longer keep it up, we collapse. Cowardice and servility are always clear indications of such degradation.

Resignation and Sadness

A contemporary German poet writes: "Things are going very well for us in this beautiful country: we are unhappy."[15] The words express with a fine irony a vehement protest against a society that seeks to satisfy the material needs of its citizens while ignoring their spiritual needs, thus crippling the expansion of their personalities.

People who have lost contact with themselves lack not just "something" but almost everything. They are without the most fundamental, basic things human beings are given: genuinely human lives—lives suited to their condition as

---

15. Martin Walser, in the poem *Hiesiger Lebenslauf*: "*Uns geht es gut im schönen Land. Wir sind unzufrieden.*"

God's beloved children whom he calls by name. The reaction to the daily pressures one experiences in life may bring about a pervasive sense of impotence because the difficulties seem too great. This can lead to resignation and bitterness.

Sadness moves us to focus too much on whatever isn't going well. This becomes the preferred subject of conversations and complaints, full of calumny and defamation of others, about even the smallest contradictions. A German proverb speaks much truth when it says: "A tongue that knows nothing but slander shows a heart that is destroyed."

Having lost contact with ourselves, we become highly sensitive and vulnerable, ready to be wounded by almost any word or gesture of another. We seek protection in the head-in-the-sand pose of ostriches, refusing to see even the slightest possibility of changing the situation so as to improve it. We constantly lament our inability to change anything around us or even within us, because everything is so wretched. But this way of deploring evil merely succeeds in reinforcing it. We end up giving evil more weight than it really has, while failing to acknowledge that, at bottom, we are excusing our own passivity.

Fears

Fear is an uncontrolled force within us. It arises in the face of danger, and it shapes our character when we have suffered injustice, ill treatment, or the hard knocks that life sends our way. Fears generate tension and anxiety, take away much of our freedom, enclose us in timidity and solitude—or, on the contrary, they may make us defensive and move us to react aggressively.

Someone who has been wounded may separate himself or herself from others, hiding his or her heart under a shell so that it appears hard, inaccessible, and untreatable. But in reality this may not be the case. It may be only doing what it must to defend itself. It may appear hard, but it is actually insecure, tormented by painful experiences. Modern man has been called a hurt child marked by anxiety and an immeasurable need for approval that is seldom received.

A fearful person fears each new day, each new situation, each new encounter. He is sure neither of himself nor his vision of the world; he lacks an ultimate support. He has yet to experience the joy of having an all-powerful Father who cares for him. He is without the serenity that comes from abandoning oneself to Divine Providence. And so he defends not his truth but his security, and he is incapable of a trusting and free relationship or of a disinterested love.

The motivation of people's lives does not always have interior freedom as its source. It may be a strategy of survival, the expression of a deeply egoistic (and barely conscious) need to please everyone, or to escape being isolated and alone. Some people feel themselves obliged to respond to each and every request (real or *imagined*) that others make of them, which leaves them exhausted. Good Christians who want to follow the example of their Lord can adopt the same attitude. But in reality they're not as free in their love as their Master, who knew how to go apart from men now and then in order to be alone with his Father. If the direction of one's life comes from one's desire for approval or the pressure of others' expectations, it can be harmful. What hinders one's development is not service, as such, but the false idea of service. No one is obliged to work without rest.

Desire for Power

Lacking a solid foundation, we are inclined to believe that being number one is the most important thing in the world and our value as persons grows as we scale the rungs of the social ladder. Someone who doesn't feel loved wants at least to be praised. On the other hand, a free man doesn't measure the chances of social success. He has higher, more interesting goals. He needs neither to dominate anyone nor prove anything to anyone.

The desire to surpass others is not rooted in strength but in weakness. Someone with little self-esteem and few convictions is easily overcome by the pressure to achieve success, to be right, to be powerful, and to be able to control everything. For such people, the world is divided into those with power and those without. Being without real strength, they seek a substitute. The man whose self-affirmation comes from dominating others is a man who has great difficulty loving: to admit that he loved someone would be to admit his need for that person, which would contradict his goal.

Pride and hardness of heart go together. Human beings in fact possess a capacity for evil that can at times be horrifying. When Albert Speer, Hitler's deputy, emerged from Spandau Prison in his old age, reporters asked him whether he considered Hitler to have been insane. "When a man goes to such extremes," he answered, "we're likely to blame it on insanity, but in fact we don't know how far the desire for power will carry a man."[16]

Not even the apostles were without feelings of superiority. "We have left everything and followed you," exclaimed Peter.[17] "And the others haven't dared to do this," he could have added. The apostles wanted to be big men in the new kingdom of God. They were confident in themselves. When

---

16. See Jose Antonio Sayés, *Teologia para nuestro tiempo* (Madrid, 1995), p. 76.
17. Mk 10:28.

the people of a certain village rejected Jesus, they were ready to call down fire from heaven to consume them.[18] How typical it is of the pharisaical mentality for the "good" to demand punishment for the "bad."

Someone who left everything could in time consider himself to be a great figure and better than others. At certain times we too are at risk of living more for our own excellence than God's glory. Yet even then God doesn't stop trusting us. On the night of Calvary, he gave his apostles the gift of purification—he destroyed their foolish illusions.[19] After that radical experience, the apostles were no longer what they'd been before—a triumphal band ready to kill all who dissented. They understood that the only one who triumphs was their Master; their triumph lay in being intimately united to him.

---

18. See Lk 9:54.

19. Heb 12:6: "The Lord disciplines him whom he loves, and chastises every son whom he receives."

✎ 8.

SCALING THE WALLS

IN THE APOCRYPHAL *Acts of Thomas* there is a story known as the "Hymn of the Pearl" that seems to be for children but is intended for adult Christians. It tells of a young man sent to Egypt by his father, an aged king of the Far East, to recover a precious pearl that is in the power of an evil serpent. Supported by his father's name and office, the young man goes with great enthusiasm on the long trip; but once in a strange land, he becomes ensnared in many worldly pursuits and allows himself to be cheated. Having consumed Egyptian delicacies, he falls into a profound lethargy, entirely forgetting who he is and why he was there. His father, worried by his delay, sends him a letter that flies in the form of an eagle. Upon reaching the young man, it is transformed into a voice that cries:

> Arise and awake from your sleep!
> Remember that you are the son of a king!
> Remember the pearl!

Rising, the young man recognizes that what the voice says coincides with what he feels in his heart, and he finally comes to his senses. He rushes to fight with the serpent, invoking his father's name; he recovers the precious pearl and heads back home.[1]

Here is a parable of our destiny. We came from God and to him we are meant to return. We are not on earth to settle down comfortably—as if life had no other purpose—but to journey toward our true homeland. While on the way, though, we are at risk of succeeding in life's secondary matters while nevertheless failing at what is fundamental, forgetting that the moments when we are applauded are not normally times of special grace.

RETURNING TO ONE'S OWN HOME

To be without external chains is not necessarily to enjoy freedom. I am free when I live at peace with myself and God.[2] But how can I disregard the judgment of men? How can I be free from dependence on external things like possessions, recognition, or security? How can I overcome the fear of failure and rejection, of sickness and death?

Literary and artistic works testify that anguish and loneliness are present in the asphalt deserts of our cities and characterize the state of mind of modern man. Life seems diminished and, more or less consciously, unsatisfactory. How did we get to this point?

The answer is within us. We have fled from our interior dwelling place where the world's problems lose their harshness and become relative. And since we are no longer

---

1. See *Acts of Thomas* (second century), in Francisco Garcia Bazán, *La gnosis eternal. Antologia de textos gnosticos* I (Madrid, 2001).

2. See St. Augustine, *On Free Will*, I, 11, 21: "No loss of physical, social or political freedom can deprive man of spiritual freedom which is his freedom to choose the good." PL 32, 1233.

at home, we find ourselves unable to open the door when God comes calling on us.

The Path to Interior Life

To return to God, we need to begin to reenter our homeland within and, from the depths of our hearts, decide to receive the strength of his grace. True freedom is a free gift of God; it is a fruit of the Spirit that we receive when we ask Jesus Christ not to leave us by ourselves, to stay with us.

Freedom, in the sense of interior maturity, is attained in a relationship with Christ. During his time on earth, he brought us freedom from prejudice and cliché, from repressive traditions and suffocating customs. He continues to act today, offering all men the gift of a new life consisting essentially in a new friendship with God.[3] He excludes no one, no matter how poor and unfortunate. He shows himself to be close to the afflicted and disheartened, the sick and ignorant, the isolated and condemned: "Come to me, all who labor and are heavy laden, and I will give you rest."[4]

What oppresses us most intimately, what demoralizes or wounds us, is first of all our own fault. How often have we thrown God out of our house![5] Pride and egoism, in their many forms, can corrode and destroy us much more deeply than external events. Christ came to free us from them. In totalitarian states those who "deviate" are placed in prison or confined to psychiatric hospitals. But in the kingdom of God, by contrast, just the reverse happens: such people are invited to a feast, the feast of forgiveness. Jesus always

---

3. See Jn 10:10.
4. Mt 11:28.
5. See 1 Cor 7:23: "You were bought at a great price; do not become slaves of men."

accepts our repentance and helps us to change.[6] "If the Son makes you free, you will be free indeed."[7]

Grace heals our wounds, raises us from the ground, and makes us feel like God's chosen daughters and sons again.[8] Through it, we feel the relief of a new beginning, a radical newness. When Jesus enters our soul, we experience a happiness we have not known before. The time of loneliness, shame, and humiliation is over. We feel we have been welcomed, restored to a dignity in which we no longer believed. We begin to see the world in a new light and to love others with a great authenticity. "He brought me forth into a broad place. . . . The Lord my God lightens my darkness."[9]

Not Living Alone

When we live conscious of that space of silence and quiet within us, no one has power over us except God. Man's complete emancipation, so much yearned for and so rarely attained, does not consist only in freeing himself from oppression and injustice in political, social, or professional life, but in severing the unhealthy dependencies that make us live in fear of the power of the world and of men—their pretensions and expectations, their judgments and condemnations.

The more you approach Jesus whom you find within you, the more fully do you become master of your life. You become increasingly conscious of a fundamental indepen-

---

6. "Do not sin again." Jn 8:11.

7. Jn 8:36; see 2 Cor 3:17; Rom 8:13–14.

8. God frees us from the slavery of sin, especially through the sacraments of baptism and penance. He frees us "from the dominion of darkness and transferred us to the kingdom of his beloved Son, in whom we have redemption, the forgiveness of sins" (Col 1:13–14), so that now "We might no longer be enslaved to sin" (Rom 6:6. See Jn 1:29; 1 Jn 1:7).

9. Ps 18:19, 28. See 1 Pet 2:9f.: God called us "out of darkness into his marvelous light."

dence with regard to this world and a fresh confidence in the life springing up from interior freedom. Then your false idols fall: You are less and less affected by the hostility or calumnies that might arise around you; you don't waste time accusing others; you don't war against anyone; you don't want to show how important you are—you simply enjoy life. There is within you a space over which no one has power, the place where God dwells. There you find great tranquility and consolation that the world cannot give you. At times, it can be encouraging to recall the words Jesus spoke to St. Catherine: "You think of me, for I will be thinking of you."

A free person has nothing to lose or defend. He is not ambitious for or fearful of anything, because all his good is in God, and there is no one above God. Why do we so eagerly seek a bit of approval or understanding from men if God wants to give us these things in abundance?

But this is no retreat into pure interiority. It is a new way of relating to others and, from this quiet place, passionately committing oneself to the world. As long as we are caught up in making comparisons, others determine the state of our soul, and we frequently feel annoyed. If, on the other hand, we are indifferent to our career path or how much money we make, if we neither have power nor desire it, then we've taken our stance outside the sphere of conventional social enmities, power plays, and rivalries. And there we can experience true communion with others.

Some people provide a clear example of how nothing external—neither isolation, nor exile, nor the loss of fortune—can really harm us. After his sentencing, Alfred Delp wrote in prison: "Finally I am a man, interiorly free and more authentic and true, more realistic than before. Now my eye finally has the ability to see all dimensions and the health to see perspectives. My shortsightedness and atrophy are being remedied."[10]

Seeking a Healthy Autonomy

Our exterior situation says very little about how we really are. A slave can be freer than his master if he retains his human dignity and a healthy spiritual autonomy. The most unscrupulous despot, on the other hand, is at best a prisoner of his passions and caprices or his courtiers' intrigues. In the old Soviet Union, people who converted to Christianity annoyed the state officials, not only by their ideas against the regime but also by the independence of their judgment and their interior elegance and greatness. In not playing their persecutors' game, they showed that they couldn't be forced to yield.[11]

The judgments of men cannot greatly impress those who live under the gaze of God. To his guards, Bonhoeffer was a surprisingly free man. Some of them came to him to tell him their problems and spent long periods of time with him, because in him they got a scent of freedom amid a world of suspicion, lies, dependency, and terror.

Jesus Christ did not provoke his detractors' opposition, but that didn't keep him from traveling the path he had to travel. Refusing to let himself be influenced by the envy of the Pharisees, he continued calmly showing his love despite the hostility surrounding him and without returning enmity for enmity with those who considered themselves his rivals.

Where God dwells within us, where we feel ourselves at home with Jesus himself, other people have no right to intrude.

10. Alfred Delp, *Letter of January 11, 1945* in idem., *Gesammelte Schriften* IV (Frankfurt, 1984), p. 107f.

11. Tatiana Goricheva, *Talking about God is Dangerous* (New York: Crossroad, 1987).

A woman may complain of being constantly humiliated by her husband or her mother-in-law or a neighbor. This aggressor becomes the sole theme of her conversation and preoccupations. She shouldn't give that person the honor of having such a powerful influence on her life—she shouldn't let him or her enter her quiet place. As a first step, what she needs to do is to separate herself from the aggressor in some way, even if only interiorly. As long as the knife is in the wound, the wound will never close. Remove the knife; get some distance from the other—only then can you see his or her face. A degree of detachment is a prerequisite to being able to forgive and extend to the other the love he or she needs. This is what also gives us the strength to swim against the current and set ourselves in opposition to unjust structures.

In this world, it's hard for someone to be just if her behavior depends on what others think of her. A man once asked St. Francis of Assisi to admit him into his new community. "It is not possible," replied the saint, "because you are not humble."

"Yes, I am," insisted the man. "I always seek the last place."

"Then," said Francis, "let's try a test: from now on, always sit in the first place and let them put you out of it, as if you were the most proud and pretentious of all. If you can do that, you can return in a year."

A person isn't defined by what others say of him, but by God. If he acts in harmony with God's will, it makes little difference whether he appears good or bad to others: he will be freer than those who criticize him.

ORDERING ONE'S OWN HOME

Attaining this interior independence isn't easy. It's a gift of God and at the same time a victory each individual must win for himself. Freedom is not static; it can increase or decrease. Personal effort to control one's self-destructive tendencies is required. The free man is the wise man who has got his passions in order.[12] St. Augustine told his young friends, "You should follow and love moderation in everything if you really want us to turn to God."[13] According to this great doctor of the Church, perfect freedom consists in abstaining from sin.[14]

The Need for an Intelligent Asceticism

Let us not be frightened by what Christian tradition has commonly called asceticism, or interior struggle. Many people consider its elements strange and uncomfortable, at odds with spontaneity, authenticity, and creativity, and they vehemently reject it. But precisely this rejection can be the reason why some lives fail.

Asceticism is indispensable for one who doesn't care to live as a "mass-man" and be manipulated by the media. We have within us a power enabling us to stand up to the blows of fate and to contemplate the stars. Today asceticism can be seen as an antidote to the threats of technological civilization. The word asceticism comes from the Greek verb *askein*, which refers to "working" and "shaping" things. It occurs only once in the New Testament, where it has the general sense of "making an effort" (to keep a clean conscience).[15] Here it signifies recovering man's original harmony.

Rather than abandoning any kind of ascetical life because of exaggerations in the past, it's necessary to

---

12. See St. Augustine, *De libero arbitrio*, I, 9,19: PL 32,1232.

13. St. Augustine, *De beata vita*, 4, 36: PL 32, 978.

14. See St. Augustine, *De Spiritu et Littera*, 16: PL 44, 218.

15. Acts 24:16.

practice it in an intelligent, prudent, and appropriate way, without coercion or fear. True dominion over oneself can only be achieved voluntarily, with great confidence and a generous heart.

Asceticism leads us to say no to many things, even licit ones, in order to overcome egoism and foster love. It makes us freer, more alert, and more responsible. It leads us to commit ourselves seriously and to keep our promises despite difficulties. And—this is fundamental—it leads to an encounter with God.

One does not seek one's own perfection by a sane asceticism, but by increased love and a fuller availability to fulfill the divine will. It is not a matter of never doing anything wrong or never falling, but of having the courage to get up again and again. Falls and defects belong to human nature. Sometimes, as a result of error or clumsiness or even a twisted intention, the falls are large and scandalous. What we do is limited and could always be much better. One who accepts the world as it is will bear all this with good humor, while acquiring an ability to criticize and correct himself. After all, God doesn't need our perfection. And surely he is better pleased when we raise our sorrowful hearts to him than when we try to flaunt our accomplishments or our irreproachable behavior.

Freeing Oneself from a False Identity

If our identity is externally imposed—not our true one, but the one we've acquired (unconsciously) in social interactions—we should dispose of it. This is a pressing task that no one can do for us. It is accomplished from within when one acquires convictions stronger and richer than the values motivating one up to that point. For example, a man who drives himself to acquire a particular social position can become more and more egocentric and hard, but as soon as he understands that his wife's love is worth far more than his position, not only his behavior but—little by little—his character as well undergoes a transformation. He becomes more authentically himself, more like the man God has always wanted him to be. "The Lord has called us to have faith, not success," said Bl. Teresa of Calcutta.

Now and then we need to get free from ourselves, from the sins and falsehoods within us. (It's no coincidence that the devil is called "the father of lies.") Sincerity is a broad and profound term. It means not only telling the truth but above all living in the truth, building one's life upon it. The "Pharisees" of every age aren't inauthentic because they lie—although they do that too—but especially because they feel self-sufficient and self-satisfied, and precisely because of this, they base their lives on a great lie.

Still, very seldom is someone altogether responsible for what he is; others have had an influence on him by their actions and judgments. If these have been negative, the effect can be unpleasant: the personality may be distorted. The French author Jo Croissant has shown the need to seek ways to confront this situation. She organizes courses to help people free themselves interiorly from dominion exerted upon them by others and to become themselves. Once she asked participants to write what they thought of themselves. This was the testimony of a young woman:

> In my room, imagining that Jesus was before me and listening to me, I began to speak, to tell him all that I thought of myself. This lasted two hours. As I expressed in words what I felt, I was more and more stupefied at hearing what came from my mouth. On the one hand, it was much more negative than I thought, while on the

other hand, I realized that it was not true. It wasn't accurate! Truly it was as if scales were falling from my eyes. I finally realized that all of the damning words that I heard and believed were false. Some were so absurd that only mentioning them was enough to "get the poison out." Others had to be reached by the sword of the Word of God, the Word of life and of blessing.[16]

Finally this woman was freed from the manipulation and pressure that came from her surroundings, free also of absurd formalisms and prohibitions. She could hear what God expected of her, and she gained the strength to begin the adventure of a new life.

Living a Simple and Serene Life

Someone who puts his confidence in God also regains, with time, his trust in humanity. One can once again see good and beauty deep down in every person, even though it might be buried in debris. On the other hand, someone who can't trust others harms himself most of all: his life is focused on himself, and he is full of fears and tensions. "One who lacks trust is old," says a proverb.

If you feel loved by God, you know you don't need to achieve everything by your own power. Thus removed from the threat of falling into activism, you begin to see the world with more depth and calm. "He who reduces his activities will become wise," as the Old Testament puts it.[17]

Saying no to power in all its forms is the beginning of virtue. A person united to Christ wants neither honor nor privilege, nor does he become overly concerned with mate-

---

16. Jo Croissant, *El cuerpo, templo de la belleza* (Buenos Aires–Mexico City, 2005), p. 71.

17. See Sir 38:24.

rial goods. He doesn't need to have everything he sees. He doesn't have to gain all that he could. He can begin to live the life God has given him. He doesn't fret constantly about what others have. He lives conscious of his divine destiny. He lives the truth.

Murillo's painting—*St. Francis embracing Christ on the Cross*—graphically expresses how far healthy disdain for earthly things can extend in the presence of God. Francis finds himself before a great crucifix. Christ has detached one of his arms and is embracing the saint, next to whom there is a globe of the earth. Francis is so enraptured that he doesn't notice that he is nudging the globe aside with his foot, as if it were nothing more than a toy.

TAKING ADVANTAGE OF "TALENTS"

We are called to trust in God. But long before that, God trusts in us. He gives us many "talents,"—gifts[18]—that we can use to make the world more beautiful and habitable.

Filling Suffering with Meaning

A "talent" can be something one has or something one lacks. In the light of faith, health is a talent but so is sickness; success is a talent but failure is even more of one.[19] "One learns little from a victory but a lot from a defeat," says a Japanese proverb. Every crisis is a source of life. Every circumstance is a gift from above, especially when it leads us to experience our deficiencies and limitations, rejections, and hard criticisms. God permits pain because he knows what he is

---

18. 1 Cor 7:17: "Let every one lead the life which the Lord has assigned to him."

19. Phil 1:29: "It has been granted to you that for the sake of Christ you should not only believe in him but also suffer for his sake."

going to do on the "third day"—the day of resurrection. If sadness is our response to a difficulty, it means we are burying a talent we have received.

Above all, we should be very careful not to toss aside the small, "undeserved" sufferings that come our way, since they join us to Christ in a very special way. Humiliations, envy, misunderstanding, and offenses of all kinds are part of a serious spiritual life. It's as if God mysteriously permits these contradictions in order to make us see what comes from the dark depths of the heart and lead us, little by little, to a humble maturity.[20] Many tales of adventure begin with some sort of lucky chance that befalls the hero but then go on to tell of the hard trials he must overcome.

Not "spoiling" the suffering means, for example, not speaking of it unless it is really necessary and indeed very useful, guarding it zealously as a secret between God and ourselves. An ancient desert father said, "No matter how great your sufferings, your victory over them will be found in silence."[21] A bishop similarly told a group of young priests on their ordination day, "You will receive many blows, but let us promise that from now on we will never return them."[22]

St. Paul thought he could proclaim Christ's message to the Corinthians with authenticity only if he were able to perform well and present himself before them as strong. But God made him see that he could use not only his strength but also his weakness and impotence while acting among them. "My grace is sufficient for you, for my power is made

---

20. See Heb 12:6: "The Lord disciplines him whom he loves, and chastises every son whom he receives."

21. *Apophthegmata Patrum*, Poemen 37: PG 65, 332.

22. See 1 Pet 3:13f: "Who is there to harm you if you are zealous for what is right? But even if you do suffer for righteousness' sake, you will be blessed. Have no fear of them, nor be troubled."

perfect in weakness."[23] Just when we touch bottom, when we've lost our hold on everything and are forced to the painful admission that we can never be sure of anything on our own, it is then that we can experience God's power. Then our strength comes from above, not from ourselves.

Bl. John Paul II did not achieve all he did despite the cross. Just the opposite: His achievements came *by* the great cross he bore—his infirmities and the physical limitations of old age. He appeared to rely more and more on the strength of God himself, whose love he transmitted steadfastly to men. "The Lord is my shepherd, I shall not want. . . . Even though I walk through the valley of the shadow of death, I fear no evil; for thou art with me; thy rod and thy staff, they comfort me."[24]

Someone who suffers is called to open himself to grace. One who does this is humble. But this is not always true of one who demeans himself. God is present where we allow him to enter and cure our wounds from within.[25] It is not necessary to "resign ourselves to God's will," as the old formula puts it, since no one resigns himself to being loved. Only someone who thinks himself self-sufficient and invulnerable has reason to be crushed in the face of misfortune; having shut himself off from life and love, he can receive nothing.

Even our sins can be turned into talents if we repent of them. They show the infinite mercy of God, who forgave David his adultery and murder, forgave the chief publican his betrayal and avarice, forgave the thief on the cross. But he did not forgive the Pharisees, for they were hypocrites and had a great sense of their own importance. They were so sure

---

23. 2 Cor 12:9.
24. Ps 23:1 and 4.
25. See Mk 1:29–39.

of themselves, so attached to their own worldview, that they couldn't tolerate criticism even coming from the Son of God. Thus they could not enjoy the freedom that comes from living with Christ and accepting one's own weakness.

Abandoning Oneself in God

Those who fully abandon themselves to God have more power than an entire army. It's not that they understand everything that happens along the way, but they trust in the goodness and wisdom of God. In this way, on days when it's raining, they can say what some Jews said during the Nazi persecution: "I believe in the sun, even when it is not shining; I believe in love, even when I do not feel it; I believe in God, even though he is silent."[26]

Sometimes, though, we're afraid to be in the minority, as if faith were strong only when confessed by millions of believers. But Christ's nearness removes doubts and fears, even as it leads us to experience the joy of our own insignificance in this world and a great optimism, the fruit of disinterested love that enables us to mobilize our energies toward the good.

Vietnamese Bishop Nguyen van Thuan expressed this state of soul in a striking poem, written during his long years in prison.

I am happy here in this cell
where white mushrooms grow
on my mat of moldy straw,
because You are with me,
because You want me to live with you.

---

26. Inscription found in a cellar where Jews were hidden from the Nazis, in John Bowker, *Religioni del mondo* (Milan, 1998), p. 113.

I have spoken much in my life.
Now I speak no more.
It is your turn to speak to me, Jesus.
I am listening to you: what have you whispered to me?
Is it a dream?

You don't speak to me of the past,
of the present;
you don't speak of my sufferings,
distresses . . .
you speak to me of your plans,
of my mission.

Then I sing of your mercy,
in the darkness, in my fragility,
in my bewilderment.

I accept my cross
and I plant it, with my two hands
in my heart.
If you were to allow me to choose, I would not change.
Because You are with me!
I am no longer afraid: I have understood. I follow You
      in your Passion
And in your Resurrection!

True peace of heart is the absence of egoism. One who loves always walks in freedom, free from his heaviest chain, free from his own ego.

Acting Courageously

Recall those ancient myths, traceable to the origins of all peoples, tales of fierce beasts that at the climactic moment are transformed into princes or princesses. Perhaps all the fierce beasts in our lives are princes or princesses just waiting to be transformed into something beautiful and brave.

In this world there are no indestructible regimes. History records cruelties and crimes, but they never have the last word. If we learn how to have interior freedom, no one but God will have power over us: "We went through fire and water; yet thou hast brought us forth."[27]

The man who follows the light of conscience is stronger than his oppressors. It doesn't matter to him if he is different from others; just by being different, he begins to change their environment, though at times he may have to pay a great price. Someone who dares to show signs of originality or to be ahead of his time can count on being "a target of hatred and jealousy of his neighbors."[28]

Nevertheless, we can always find outstanding persons who refuse to sell their freedom for gold or to give in under the lash. So, for example, the prophet Nathan dared to speak truth to an adulterous, murderous king.[29] St. John the Baptist might have died in a comfortable bed had he not told Herod what he thought of him. Something similar might be said of St. Thomas More, who went to his death for refusing to subscribe to the laws of Henry VIII.

The history of Christianity has been filled from the beginnings with testimonies of heroism. In Athens and in Rome, those who didn't burn incense before the statues of the national gods were treated as enemies of the people. Absurd as their worship often was, the ancient pagan state religions imposed submission on all citizens. The first

---

27. Ps 66:12.
28. Adam, *La virtud de la libertad*, cit., p. 257.
29. See 1 Kings 12:1f.

Christian epoch witnessed a continuous struggle for religious freedom against the intolerance of a corrupted state and a people poisoned by prejudice.[30]

The martyrs of all centuries placed unlimited faith and confidence in God. "The Lord is my rock, and my fortress, and my deliverer."[31] Based on these examples, Christianity soon became a bastion of freedom. It attracted courageous people who fled mediocrity. "That is how St. Clement of Alexandria could write with calm enthusiasm that 'it is a beautiful adventure to go voluntarily into the camp of God.' The pagan Horace had hinted at this already in his own way when he said: 'to follow God is a sweet risk.'"[32]

It is worth taking this risk and living one's life with courage. Christ doesn't summon us to a bourgeois existence. He doesn't mean for us to live in a zoo, with bars, cages, and barriers. The life he prepares for us is much more exciting. Yes, it leads us into a jungle full of dangers. But, supported at each moment by God's almighty power, we should fear nothing and no one: "By my God I can leap over a wall."[33]

---

30. See John Henry Newman, *Callista* (London, 1901; orig. 1855).

31. Ps 18[17]:2.

32. Clement of Alexandria, *Protreptico* 10, 93, 2. Horace, *Ode* III, 25, 18–19; both cited in Morales Marín, *Virgo veneranda*, in *Scripta de Maria* VIII (1985), p. 432f.

33. Ps 18 [17]:29.

ᗌ9.

CREATING FREE ENVIRONMENTS

SOME CHRISTIANS PREFER THE PATH of law to the paths of freedom.[1] To reach the goal, they say, one does better to stick to the safety of preset rules than at each moment decide for oneself what ought to be done. See how many sins one avoids that way! Aren't they right? Don't we often use our strength badly? Aren't the worst revolutions born under the sign of freedom?

Looking about us, we see few people who understand the radical newness of the Gospel—the great liberation worked by Christ—and still fewer who are capable of fully benefiting from it. Apparently we can't do the right thing apart from controls and warnings.[2]

Yet God knows our weaknesses better than we do, and he has always known that we would abuse our best gifts. But despite that, he did not wish to take away our

---

1. Understood correctly, the paths of the law and of freedom are not opposed to each other.

2. There are even some who think that it is the task of the state to guide its subjects so that they do not commit errors; for this, freedom has to be reduced. And this is "preached" from all political trenches.

freedom; and, still more, he made freedom the distinctive sign of the Christian.[3]

THE LEGEND OF THE GRAND INQUISITOR

Dostoyevsky deals with this subject in the episode in his celebrated novel *The Brothers Karamazov* called the Legend of the Grand Inquisitor. Ivan, one of the brothers, invented the legend and is telling it to the youngest brother, Alyosha, presenting the problem in an extreme, even melodramatic form by setting it in the context of a confrontation between the cardinal-inquisitor and Jesus.[4]

The action takes place in sixteenth-century Seville during "the most horrible time of the Inquisition, when fires blazed every day to the glory of God." The day after a bloody *auto da fe* in which "almost a hundred heretics" were burned,[5] the Savior visits the streets of the city with a smile of infinite compassion. The people recognize him at once, flock to his side, cry with joy, and kiss the places where he has walked. When he revives a dead girl at the entrance to the cathedral, they applaud wildly.

At that precise moment the Grand Inquisitor arrives. "He is an old man, almost ninety, tall and straight, with a gaunt face and sunken eyes."[6] Witnessing the popular enthusiasm, he puckers his bushy eyebrows, extends his withered hand, and orders the guards to arrest Jesus. The

---

3. See Ratzinger (Benedict XVI), *Introduction to Christianity* (Ignatius Press, 2000).

4. See Fyodor Dostoyevsky, *The Brothers Karamazov* (New York: Alfred Knopf, 1992), pp. 248–262. One has to take into account that this is a religious caricature.

5. Ibid., p. 248.

6. Ibid., p. 249.

crowd, terrorized and so accustomed to obeying the inquisitor, moves aside and the order is carried out.

The Savior is locked in a gloomy, vaulted prison in the ancient palace of the tribunal of the Inquisition. When night has fallen, the door of the cell opens and the grand inquisitor enters carrying a torch. After closing the door with great caution, he gazes into the face of the holy prisoner and begins to insult him with a growing nervousness: "Why have you come to interfere with us now? . . . Don't you know that we have improved your work? . . . Repeating that you made your followers free, you have intoxicated them with dangerous illusions. For freedom only serves to make men unhappy. . . . Haven't you seen these people? They tremble in the face of freedom; they don't understand it, nor know what benefit they can get from it. Freedom is the most insufferable thing in this world. . . . " Jesus listens without saying a word.[7]

Then, recalling a scene from the Gospel, the grand inquisitor tells his prisoner it would have been better for him to have listened to the tempter when he offered him bread, miracles, and power. How much more happy would men have been with those gifts than with that fateful freedom! "If you had taken the world and Caesar's purple, you would have founded the universal state and have given universal peace. For who can rule men if not he who holds their conscience and their bread in his hands?"[8]

Fortunately, continues the inquisitor, Christ's mistakes have been corrected by his ecclesiastical representatives. These behave so shrewdly that the people themselves hand them their freedom on a tray. They would rather be ruled

7. Ibid., p. 252f.
8. Ibid., p. 254f.

than have to confront their own responsibility. "Millions of human beings now feel themselves exempt from the torment of freedom. Why have you come then to disturb us? I myself will command that you be burned alive tomorrow. I have spoken."[9]

Christ is content to turn a penetrating gaze upon the indignant cardinal. Suddenly, without saying a word, he approaches him and gives him a kiss. It is his only answer! The cardinal trembles. He goes to the door, opens it violently, and cries, "Leave at once, and don't come back, never again!" So ends the legend. . . .

Alyosha has followed the narration with close attention. At the end, he says sorrowfully to his brother, "Your inquisitor does not believe in God! There's no other explanation." Ivan replies, "You have guessed it. It's perfectly true."[10]

Indeed, one who doesn't accept freedom does not trust in God and perhaps does not believe in him. Underlying the idea that human beings redeemed by Christ are incapable of freedom is an atheistic pessimism. But with the poet Angelus Silesius, we can also affirm the opposite truth: "Whoever loves freedom, loves God."[11]

On one occasion Pope Benedict XVI observed: "I think that we have really been able to see that God has entered into history in a much more fragile way, so to speak, than we would like. But also that this is his answer to freedom. And if we want God to respect freedom and approve of it when he does, then we must also learn to respect and love the

---

9. Ibid., p. 260.
10. Ibid., p. 261.
11. See Aquinas, *Summa Contra Gentiles*, 3, 69: "One who does not recognize that creatures have an activity proper to them sins against the goodness of God."

fragility of his action."[12] A little later, the Pope added: "This is, of course, exactly the question that I, too . . . would ask. . . . Why does he remain so powerless? Why does he reign only in this curiously weak way, as a crucified man, as one who himself failed? But apparently that is the way he wants to rule; that is the divine form of power. And the non-divine form of power obviously consists in imposing oneself and getting one's way and coercing."[13]

SUFFOCATING LIFE AND FREEDOM

In the Legend of the Grand Inquisitor, Dostoyevsky explained Christ's "failure" as consisting precisely in giving mankind freedom: men preferred eating their bread in slavery to the tremendous effort involved in taking responsibility for their lives. This dark aspect of the human condition is already clearly visible in the Old Testament. At various times during their journey in the desert, the people of Israel wanted to return to Egypt—to the security the Pharaoh gave them—rather than continue the risky adventure of freedom.[14]

Instilling Fear

How many people realize—perhaps at an advanced age— that they haven't really lived, haven't been protagonists of their lives? As the women in the chorus say in T.S. Eliot's *Murder in the Cathedral,* they've passed through life "half alive."[15] And then there are those who don't let others live, tormenting them with an endless stream of rules and com-

---

12. Ratzinger [Benedict XVI], *The Salt of the Earth: Christianity and the Catholic Church at the End of the Millennium* (San Francisco, 1997), p. 220.
13. Ibid., p. 221.
14. See Num 11:4–15.
15. See T. S. Eliot, *Murder in the Cathedral* (New York, 1935).

mands that suffocate their souls and their desire to live. Tacitus, the famous Roman historian, spoke of this: "The more laws the state issues, the worse it governs."[16]

Throughout history one can observe signs of an inability to conceive of religion in any terms except fear—the fear of punishment. But this fear breeds a narrow mentality, even as it expresses a feeble piety. It's the piety of someone who doesn't feel free and, taking no pleasure at the thought of a God who is constantly judging him, is easily overwhelmed or depressed. Only love empowers us to live faith freely and joyfully, as God expects of us.[17]

Superfluous, damaging rules can also be laid down in God's name.[18] At times "there arises the danger of thoughtlessly, mercilessly invading the conscience of others."[19] People who retain a free spirit in such circumstances are suspect. Sometimes they are the victims of "a campaign of slurs on [their] name, defamation of [their] . . . conduct." Jesus Christ himself suffered this "biting and wounding criticism," as did those who followed him.[20] "The hour is coming when whoever kills you will think he is offering service to God."[21] Our Lord's statement has been abundantly verified over the centuries. We need to understand at a deep level that God has left us free even to offend him and condemn ourselves. We cannot force anyone to be good, since that is the task of each individual. (Teaching others to be

---

16. "*Pessima respublica plurimae leges.*"

17. See Col 3:14.

18. Of course, there are moral bulwarks that constitute the indispensable safeguards of authentic freedom. But they should not suffocate life.

19. St. Josemaría Escrivá, "Christian Respect for the Person and his Freedom," in *Christ Is Passing By* (New York: Scepter Publishers, 2002), no. 67.

20. Ibid.

21. Jn 16:2.

good is one thing, forcing them quite another.) A system that represses freedom of conscience may tame many turbulent spirits, but at the same time it prevents much good. And above all, it does not fulfill God's will.

Manipulating Knowledge

An authoritarian person need not be unpleasant. He may love others very much, and although he dominates them, they are pleased with it. He is ready to give them everything ("bread and circuses") except freedom. Often, therefore, his subjects flock to him and make him an object of their adulation.

Any time a great crisis of authority has arisen, says August Adam, it has been because "those who hold power lack the gift of discernment, and consider as diehard revolutionaries anyone who speaks the truth frankly and honorably, while they gladly listen to and favor the adulator who is eager for advancement."[22] It is the folly of a tyrant to bar all dissent and refuse ever to admit his errors for fear of losing his putative authority. In this manner, he conceals his own insecurity.

Truth has no value in totalitarian systems. Rulers declare the truth to be whatever suits them. Lies and treachery reign. Consciences are manipulated by false, restricted information and slanted news reports; strict control is imposed upon the organs of culture. People are not allowed to say what they think and live according to the truth as they understand it. In this way they are demeaned and disrespected, their personal dignity is taken away, and often they are transformed into a homogeneous mass, tired and sad, lacking any initiative of their own.

---

22. Adam, *La virtud de la libertad*, cit., p. 114f.

What devalues man is not so much economic dependence in its varied forms but the loss of personal rights.[23] When he notices this loss, a man's whole life becomes paralyzed. Even though he may produce many useful things for society, the man without freedom, the dependent man, becomes more and more sluggish in his interior life. Particularly unfortunate is the one who resigns himself to this state of abuse, taking it as natural to lack convictions of his own and always to bow before those in power. "He becomes a contemptible automaton. He has no character, and isn't capable of honesty and fidelity; he is ignorant of the meaning of truth and courage."[24]

Certain ideological systems, arbitrarily constructed by men, need the power of the authorities in order to triumph because they are false. To live the faith fully, however, one doesn't need a mule driver or harness to keep one in line; the power of grace is enough. While well aware, in the presence of God, that it is more comfortable to be on the side of the powerful and confident, we know that Christ didn't take his stance there.

Isolating People

Some boarding schools in the past made it a practice to keep students isolated from one another in order to have more influence and control over them than when they were joined together in groups in solidarity.[25] In addition, a one-directional loyalty to the directors was demanded of them,

---

23. In reality, one goes hand in hand with the other: economic freedom has rightly been called "everyday democracy." Without it one cannot have free development, as we have seen so often in history.

24. Adam, *La virtud de la libertad,* cit., p. 46.

25. This is the old "*divide et impera* (divide and conquer.)"

while no such loyalty to their companions was permitted. This approach may have had praiseworthy educational aims, but it sometimes did great harm.

Romano Guardini tells how, in his days as a seminarian, he and a friend sometimes discussed matters about which they had their own opinions. Learning of those conversations, the rector called them to order and severely punished them: he and his friend were ordained six months after their classmates. "All of this showed such an absolute lack of trust and of friendship, a lack of sincerity, openness, and uprightness that, even today, after thirty-five years, I still cannot understand it."[26]

Actually, when the open exchange of feelings, thoughts, or simple impressions is prohibited, one can, even with good intentions, create an asphyxiating atmosphere that suffocates freedom. We must take into account that the pedagogy that God asks us to use in leading others to maturity varies according to the mentality and circumstances of different eras.

Too-close supervision that doesn't know how to give freedom and space to operate stifles motivation and responsibility. It fosters an atmosphere of apathy, passivity, gloom, and timidity. Formation then produces only slaves or rebels or, in the best case, a mediocre "law-abiding person," while education promotes the unnatural and unhealthy development of students.

Repressed conflicts can erupt at any moment. Someone who is unaccustomed to acting freely won't be able to do so when liberated. With good reason Schiller says: "Never fear a free man; but quake before the slave if he manages to burst his chains." It has been shown repeatedly that people

---

26. Romano Guardini, *Apuntes para una autobiografía* (Madrid, 1991), p. 134.

raised in an extremely rigid manner often live like libertines when they come of age.

Never suppress freedom—this was the teaching of St. Josemaría Escrivá. On one occasion, around the middle of the last century, the parents of a student, seeking a "safe" place in Madrid for their son, visited a residence of Opus Dei. When they invited Escrivá to take charge of the boy so that he wouldn't be "lost" in the big city, they got a very clear answer: "You have come to the wrong door. Here we don't keep watch on anyone. In this house we love freedom very much, and anyone who is not capable of living it, and of respecting that of the others, has no place among us."[27]

ACCEPTING LIFE AS A GIFT

God doesn't want robots; he desires friends. He invites us to accept his gifts, but he never forces us. He has chosen the path of friendship, which is slower, but also more respectful of freedom and the rhythms of our nature.

Accepting Dangers

Pope Benedict XVI speaks of the element of adventure in the redemption worked by Christ, which is always related to freedom. "Redemption is . . . never imposed from the outside or cemented by firm structures but is held in the fragile vessel of human freedom. If we believe that human nature has attained a higher level, we have to reckon with the fact that it can all collapse. This, I would say, is nothing less than the conflict that Jesus settles in his temptations:

---

27. See St. Josemaría, *Friends of God*, "Give everyone the utmost credit for what he says. Be very noble." Francisco Ponz, *Mi encuentro con el Fundador del Opus Dei* (Pamplona, 2000), no. 159; p. 74.

Must redemption be something that stands permanently as a structure in the world and that can then be calculated quantitatively: Everyone has gotten bread, from now on there is no more hunger? Or is redemption something quite different? Because it is bound to freedom, because it is not something that is already imposed in structures but again and again appeals to freedom, which in turn makes it to a certain degree vulnerable."[28]

Freedom is a risk. So is love. To live up to the divine plan for us, which means living as human beings, we mustn't renounce either of them. Sin consists not only in doing bad things but also in omitting good things—not acting, not being alive, for fear of making mistakes.[29] Yes, the powerful yearning for freedom in people today may contain a considerable admixture of deception leading at times to mistaken paths. But at its core there is always something healthy and noble.

President Pinochet of Chile once asked Bl. John Paul II: "Why is the Church always talking about democracy? One method of government is as good as another." The Pope answered, "No, the people have a right to their liberties, even if they make mistakes in exercising them."[30]

There are always dangers, but those who live freely as Christians do not overemphasize them. Instead they fix their eyes upon a high goal worth living and suffering for.

---

28. Ratzinger, (Benedict XVI), *The Salt of the Earth: The Church at the End of the Millennium*, p. 219.

29. Cf. Adam, *La Virtud de la Libertad*: "It's been said that 'one must take a risk with young people in order to bring forth men.' More than one will get worn out and even die; but that is preferable to having a whole generation educated for slavery and humiliation for fear of the bad use of freedom, as if one could only abuse freedom and never legal authority." Cit., p. 175.

30. George Weigel, *Witness to Hope: The Biography of Pope John Paul II* (New York, 1999), p. 533.

Marching, it has been said, is hard on the boots but healthy for the marchers.

Engendering Trust and Joy

Every human community—from the smallest to the United Nations—should be a realm of liberty. If it isn't, don't ask the authorities why—ask the outcasts and the sick. Often they have a better understanding of what needs to be changed and improved than do the "well-adjusted."

A relationship with another person can be for us a source of life and growth—or of sickness and paralysis; to be with another can make us good or bad, happy or sad. All of us need the experience of being loved unconditionally, and someone who does not have this experience does not love. If he feels treated as an object, he will treat others in the same way; if he has been exploited, he will exploit others.

If we must regularly hide our weaknesses for fear of being judged badly, our contact with others will inevitably be at a very superficial level. Whatever truly interests us, makes us suffer, keeps us awake, or moves us to sadness or compassion, what stirs up our gratitude or our sorrow—in a word, whatever is present in the depths of the soul—will not enter into our human relationships. And as a result, these relationships become ever less stimulating and more artificial.

By contrast, where trust reigns, there are no unnecessary rules and regulations. No one forces anyone else to act according to what suits him; everyone's convictions and particular paths are respected—and so everyone feels valued and accepted. No need to close oneself off and defend oneself against the others: people can remove their armor, open their hearts wide, and allow others to enter into intimacy with them.[31]

Where there is trust, we encounter others authentically and speak frankly of whatever we wish. These fundamental rights are characteristic of freedom.[32] There are no forbidden truths; all that is forbidden is to speak the truth in a bitter way that lacks charity. Bl. John Paul II recalled his days as a bishop in Poland: "There were also separate meetings with the clergy. I wanted to give an opportunity to each of them to confide in me, to share the joys and concerns of their particular ministry. I greatly valued these meetings; they enabled me to learn from the treasury of wisdom accumulated over many years of apostolic labor."[33]

When we experience the sincere trust of others, knowing that they believe in something good and beautiful in us, despite all our faults, a profound joy is awakened in our hearts. Having someone look at us with affection moves us to undertake great things because we want to deserve that look.

Some people create an atmosphere of trust and joy around themselves. It's as if they give wings to others. They establish great vital spaces where all can develop themselves with joy and personal initiative. The world seems broader and wider; life looks more beautiful; and in this way human beings are led to make full use of their personal freedom.

---

31. I Jn 4:18: "Perfect love casts out fear."

32. There is a "rhetoric of freedom" as opposed to a "rhetoric of slavery" (Ratzinger), characterized by adulation, avarice, and pride and making one impure before God.

33. Bl. John Paul II, *Rise, Let Us Be On Our Way* (New York: Warner Books, 2004), p. 76.

≈10.

EDUCATING FREE PERSONS

NATURE REQUIRES FREEDOM TO DEVELOP. If there are no obstacles, plants will grow and flourish splendidly, and animals will roam the forests, prairies, mountains, jungles, and seas. But this is true only up to a certain point. Gardening can turn random underbrush into useful growth and cultivate an apple tree so that it gives more fruit. Under a trainer's instruction, a dog becomes the faithful watchman of a country house, or the children's good friend. Wise direction of natural forces can make the world more beautiful and livable.

What is true of flowers or birds is still more applicable to human beings: a little care works marvels; neglect can be dangerous. But apart from this, education is nothing like gardening or dog training, since the subjects here are free individuals called to an eternal life of love and happiness.

No one can reach fulfillment without help and direction from others. No one could ever create himself or herself. We owe our origin to others. Our self-realization requires others. The importance of education in the process is even more apparent when we reflect on the fact that our nature is marred by sin.[1] The intellect needs enlightenment; the will must be strengthened; feelings must be purified of egoism. "Those in charge of education can reasonably be expected to give young people instruction respectful of the truth, the qualities of the heart, and the moral and spiritual dignity of man."[2] In this great task, parents and teachers should eliminate all that could diminish or demean children, but their freedom can never be eliminated without offending gravely human nature. It is not easy to bring someone to free and responsible obedience—obedient freedom—but it is worth making the effort. St. John Chrysostom rightly says, "I appreciate one who knows how to form the heart of young people more than a painter, or a sculptor, or the greatest of artists."[3]

START WITH THE TEACHER

More important than this or that specific way of acting is the teacher, himself. A good teacher has more influence by his or her life than by his or her lessons. Teachers are the way by which others, observing them, find themselves. As the old saying goes, "Seek a teacher whom you can appreciate more for what you see of him than for what you hear from him." In his youth, Bl. John Paul II encountered a teacher of this kind; he once said: "My father demanded so much of himself that he didn't have to demand anything from me."

We transmit what we think, but above all we transmit what we are. What really moves, convinces, impacts, and

---

1. See Rom 5:12, 19. CCC, 407.
2. CCC, 2526.
3. John Chrysostom, *Comment in Mathaeum*, ch. 18, Homily 60.

stimulates is the personality of the other. It's said that one day a desperate mother sought out a rabbi with a reputation as a wise man and asked him, "What can I do? My son is totally dependent on his companions. All day he compares himself with them and does what they decide. He has no will of his own. How can I change him?" The rabbi answered: "You don't have to change your son but yourself. Your son's problems reflect your own. Change yourself!"

To be sure, this recommendation cannot and should not be applied to every family having trouble with children. That would be extremely unfair, since our society is full of more or less hidden agents of education. But it can be applied to a generation as a whole. Young people often clearly express the deep-rooted attitudes of adults: if they enjoy greater interior freedom and have a healthy independence from their surroundings, it will make a difference in the children—they will be more independent and freer.

Therefore, it is good that we become more aware of our responsibility. Everything we do has an influence on our surroundings. Let us not complain about the subliminal coercion found in competitive consumerist societies, for we are the ones who have created them—or at least kept them going. At times, one sees really ridiculous things: success identified with a perfume, or freedom with dying one's hair green (no longer so original these days). We need to escape manipulation, show our uniqueness, and acquire our own lifestyle. Someone with the courage to go against the current without becoming hard or looking down on others can carry many along with him.

Educators are also children of their times. Their effectiveness in directing others requires them to be able to discern the true and valuable from what is mere glitz and propaganda. They needn't be perfect, but they must be authentic. It doesn't matter if they have defects and weaknesses; these can even make them more likable. But they should be struggling sincerely, and with a positive outlook, to overcome their false dependence.

LOVING EACH ONE AS UNIQUE

We feel strong and free when we know that we are loved unconditionally, without reference to our merits and talents, to what we've accomplished or hope to accomplish. We feel happy when someone says to us, "I love you for what you are, not first or even second for your beauty or your intelligence, your riches or your musical talent. You can count on me through all the ups and downs of life."

A Love that Liberates

Love is crucial to the health and development of every human being from birth to death. A certain ruler in the past, wanting to know what language a child would speak to whom no one had ever spoken, sought out newborn infants who had been abandoned, placed them in a well-equipped hospital, and gave the nurses strict orders to provide well for their feeding and hygiene but never speak to them or look or smile at them or show them any affection. In a word, they were to act like "automatons" so that the babies would not grow to like them. Thus the ruler hoped to discover the original language of humankind. But instead of speaking, the infants became weaker and weaker, sickened, and eventually died.

Early in life every child makes a basic discovery, of vital importance to his character: Either "I am important, they understand and love me" or "I am in the way, I am a nuisance." The care of an affectionate person forms children who are stable, affectionate, and responsible. But if such care is lacking, the children may become incapable of establishing relationships or working seriously. Above all, they cannot use their freedom properly.

The more we love children, the better their development and the greater their trust in the world around them. But this love must not be binding and inhibiting; it must permit them to be fully *other*—that is, truly free. Some people act like the tavern keeper Procrustes in Greek mythology, who "adjusted" his guests to fit his beds: if too small, he stretched their arms and legs; if large, he would cut off their extremities. Similarly, we do violence to tulips if we treat them like oaks.

When a child's uniqueness isn't respected, he reacts with distrust, feels interiorly wounded, and closes himself off, unable to develop a healthy consciousness of his own dignity and incapable of opening up to others. Perhaps he has a shocking egoism, but it's unhealthy: he must *have* more to *be* more. "The history of the failure of every man or woman speaks of a marvelous child, highly esteemed, very special, and with many good qualities, who has lost a sense of his own value."[4]

But the child who respects his or her originality can acquire a happy self-esteem that makes education possible. Cold iron can't be molded, but it can be easily shaped when it is heated. A climate of acceptance, where love stimulates the best in others, awakens the desire to learn. Freedom grows to the extent that true knowledge about God and the world is transmitted, and those being educated are taught to make their minds the guide of their conduct.

---

4. See John Bradshaw, *Das Kind in Uns* (*The Child in Us*), cit., p. 66.

Accommodating the mystery of the irreducible *other-ness* of a person is not the same thing as mistaken permissiveness. Freedom does not consist in allowing oneself to be led by the impulse of the moment. On the contrary: a free man is not a prisoner of his whims or his surroundings—his feelings in their most superficial aspect. He is one who makes just decisions (even when out of sorts)—and who can direct his life toward a great goal that does not vary according to circumstances.

A Love that Accompanies

Some parents prefer security to vitality. Seemingly not wanting their children to leave childhood, they continue to instruct them long after they should be traveling earth's pathways on their own. Indeed, accepting the risk of one's children's freedom is one of the sharpest trials parents undergo. They'd like to spare their offspring all pain and evil, but they need to understand that this isn't possible. In walling up their children in an ivory tower, they do them a sad disservice: they may prevent the tears, but also the laughter and joy. They keep the children from experiencing life and becoming mature.

"Fathers, do not provoke your children, lest they become discouraged.[5] Interpreting this text, St. Thomas says that in requiring too strict an obedience from others, one makes them timid and retiring.[6] A person constantly treated as a child loses confidence in himself or the teacher and becomes hypocritical or stubborn as temperament dictates.

This doesn't mean, though, that parents should surrender to their children's caprices. They can and should set rea-

---

5. Col 3:21.
6. See Aquinas, *Comment in Col.*, ch. 3.

sonable limits as determined by the age and circumstances of each. Profoundly respecting a child's freedom doesn't mean distancing oneself from him to the point of indifference. It means teaching him to live in accord with his dignity as a free being, making decisions and being responsible for his own actions.

In a successful and healthy family, the virtue of acceptance is joined to that of care. Good parents accept their children in their originality and also stand by them in their doings, even in their failures and mistakes. When young people seem to be leaving the right path, parents can look to the risen Jesus, who walked patiently in the wrong direction with the disciples of Emmaus. Moved by a long conversation with the Savior, the two disciples who had fled from Jerusalem returned with new enthusiasm to Peter and the other apostles.[7]

We can never grant as much freedom as God grants us. He has infinitely more confidence in us than we do.

EXERCISING A HEALTHY AUTHORITY

Some teachers achieve a certain prestige by making others obey and fear them. If we look more closely, however, we see that their students' obedience is limited to carrying out orders they've received; it is extorted by means of strict vigilance on the teacher's part. There is no love, and so what is taught remains on the surface; it doesn't touch hearts or transform from within. "A teacher who knows nothing more than to inculcate obligations into the child (without ever saying a word about his rights), will perhaps form submissive people, but with very few convic-

---

7. See Lk 24:13–35.

tions and of little initiative. Fear of one's superiors kills all love and all enthusiasm. Undoubtedly, slaves obey quicker than free men and it is more comfortable—although less satisfactory—to command the former. But who doesn't see that such obedience is empty of merit since it is not deep nor can it be lasting."[8]

He who fears is not perfect in charity, but neither is one who causes fear. "You murder souls by strictness," said St. Teresa. A severe way of acting exercises the least elevated and suppresses the noblest feelings in the student. These so-called "teachers" lack, in addition, personal dignity, because they do not respect the dignity of their students—they assert themselves by demeaning them.

Helping Others to Grow

The word authority is highly unpopular because for many it conjures up memories of coercion. But it's a mistake to confuse *authority* with *authoritarianism*. The Latin etymology of the word suggests just the opposite, in no way expressing one person's determination to keep another in a state of perpetual childishness. The noun *authority* comes from the verb *augere*, meaning "to increase" or "to make grow." An authority is someone who makes others grow, not a weighty burden inhibiting development.

The encounter with true authority broadens and exalts a person rather than suffocating or repressing him. It helps one go ahead on the right path, be more and more oneself, and give God the glory that can be given only individually. The Gospel tells us of the reaction of the Jews who first observed Jesus at the start of his public life: "And they were astonished at his teaching, for he taught them as one

---

8. Adam, *La virtud de la libertad,* cit., p. 300.

who had authority."[9] Like their Master, the apostles also wanted to exercise their authority only to increase the joy of others.[10]

To command is to serve, not to dominate. This service is to the other in all dimensions of his being, from the most material to the most spiritual. A person is happy in knowing that others count on him and allow him to participate—gradually—in decisions made within a family, a community, or a business. There is a stage play in which an employee tells his boss in disappointment: "I offer you collaboration, and all you ask of me is obedience." Wouldn't many adolescents say the same to their parents and teachers?

Allowing Corrections

To encourage obedience, it's good to explain, insofar as possible, the reasons behind a particular decision. The truth makes us free, and it should be shown, not imposed.[11] Parents therefore should make it a habit to speak with their children in a manner suited to the capacity of each; they should explain their motives simply and hear out the children's arguments to the end, alert to what is *not* said, that which is kept inside and may be the most important thing.

It isn't advisable for educators to try at all costs to avoid any conflict, arranging things so they don't suffer even the slightest contradiction. If they ban criticism on principle and require the youngsters to be silent about what they don't understand or accept, they may get an interval of apparent peace, but soon they will pay a very high price. The young

---

9. Mk 1:22.
10. See 2 Cor 1:24:
11. See *DH* 1; UUS 3.

people will stop telling them what's really bothering them and will lull them with superficial talk. Avoiding conflict is avoiding contact: a closing off of the self from a trusting, friendly relationship.[12]

The etymological meaning of the word "criticize" isn't contradicting or murmuring. The word *critic* comes from the Greek *krinein*—to judge or to discern for oneself true and false, right and wrong, good and bad. One can conclude from this that true criticism is a very worthwhile quality—even a Christian virtue—which every mature person should have. Everyone should be able to choose the good with full knowledge and to argue with those who think differently.[13] (We have to be respectful of the opinions and feelings of others, of course, but without renouncing our own views.)

Educators who understand that there are healthy rebellions against hypocrisy and duplicity, against haughtiness, formalism, and manipulation, who are able to ask pardon of young people for their own faults and blunders (and there will always be some), who are ready to learn from everyone—educators like this exercise their authority with maturity. They grow interiorly to the point of being able to look at their own position from the outside and allow themselves to be corrected. "To be parents it is necessary to continue being children."[14]

---

12. See 1 Cor 11:19: "There must be factions among you in order that those who are genuine among you may be recognized."

13. St. Paul demanded of adult Christians that they have "their faculties trained by practice to distinguish good from evil" (Heb 5:14). He listed the "gift of discernment" among the great charisms of the Holy Spirit. See 1 Corinthians 12:10. In the same way, his principle, "Test everything; hold fast what is good" (1 Thess 5:21), requires a great capacity for discernment.

14. Angelo Scola, *La cuestion decisiva del amor: hombre-mujer* (Madrid, 2003), p. 97.

WITH UNDERSTANDING AND HUMILITY

We should keep in mind that everyone needs more love than he "deserves," that we are all more vulnerable than we seem, that we are all weak and can grow tired. No matter how egoistical and scandalous a person's behavior is, a good teacher can see someone tenderly loved by God. He is firmly convinced that behind every façade is a human being who is vulnerable and capable of changing. He knows that a great destiny awaits everyone.

Helping in Times of Failure

When someone behaves badly, he should be corrected. While everyone has a duty in this matter, it is particularly pressing for those who educate young people. If parents don't correct their children—through indifference, laziness, a certain fear of "losing them," a false notion of freedom, or a fear that they will be hurt—they can do great harm. They may make the child blind toward values, without a sense of direction in their lives. Indignation, even anger, are normal reactions—and in certain situations even necessary. To respect the uniqueness of another does not require closing one's eyes to injustices or denying that sins are sins.

One of the distinctive features of people today is their lack of awareness of their faults. It is clearer than ever that such awareness doesn't come from teaching moral norms emphatically or rigorously dictating their application. Failing to observe an external law can make someone fearful or sad, but it does not move one to heartfelt guilt. This sensitivity is acquired only in a relationship with another person, a relationship of love. Christian educators, therefore, aim to help young people "let themselves be taken and conquered by the luminous figure of Jesus Christ."[15] They want them to encounter God. Someone who loves always feels himself to be a debtor, obliged to respond ever more generously and lovingly to the one whom he loves, yet simultaneously unable to give all he would wish because the one loved always deserves much more. To be sure, once an awareness of guilt awakens, it orients itself according to ethical norms; but its deepest source is not these norms, but love.

If someone acts badly, it is necessary to tell him or her so. But it's equally important to find the right moment and a suitable manner and tone for correction. Harsh, rock-hard truth can give rise to hatred.

How truth is spoken is as important as what the truth is, and this will be different for each person and situation. There are no set formulae or ready-made solutions; everyone is different, with his or her own needs and feelings. One young person's clear, precise warning can be for another an unbearable reproach that plunges him or her into misery. Sometimes it can be profoundly disturbing to a person to have attention called to some personal fault. The wise, healthy thing to do in this case would be to cover the fault with silence. There are moments when there is no right thing to say and no possibility of understanding what is said.

Still, whatever the particular circumstance, it's good to communicate to those who make mistakes the fact that we still have full confidence in them, just as others have confidence in us despite our wretchedness. "No, you're not like that. I know you, and you're really much better." Precisely when a person has failed, he needs to experience the reality of having someone else that loves him and desires for him

---

15. Bl. John Paul II, Address (October 16, 1979).

everything that is good, his full development, and his deep happiness. He needs to know that someone loves him from the bottom of his or her heart, with great sincerity.

One denies another person the space he needs to live and breathe by failing to see the good that is in him. In this way the person is progressively cut off from the realization of his self-ideal. Spiritually speaking, this is how to kill him. This kind of death is inflicted by unjust, harsh words, by bad thoughts, or simply by refusing forgiveness. Then the other person may become sad and filled with bitterness. Kierkegaard speaks of the desperation of one who "desperately wants to be himself" and cannot because others prevent it.[16]

The educator's task is to look deeply and discern what young people want to express through their errant behavior. Is it a need for attention arising from loneliness? Is it boredom, depression, desperation? Do they see any meaning in life? It's wrong to judge others. We can't perceive the depths of the human heart, and if we knew what was hidden there, we'd be more than slightly surprised. At the same time, we must take into account that a living person is constantly changing (and changing even more if divine grace is at work). Thus, we can't "classify" or put anyone in a box. It would be as if a pilot prepared to take off by reading last week's weather report.

Avoiding Rigorism

Psychology teaches us that people can break down if continual demands are made on them for "more of the same"—more work, higher marks, more speed, more

---

16. Kierkegaard, *Die Krankheit zum Tode*, (*Sickness unto Death*) (München, 1976), p. 99.

money, more production. It's good to use your abilities, but becoming obsessed with results can be dangerous. Discipline undoubtedly ennobles, but exaggerated discipline robs a man of vigor and strength and hastens his decline. There's an ancient Chinese saying that says, "Hardness and rigidity are qualities of death, flexibility and gentleness qualities of life."

If someone dealing with young people insists on pounding them with precepts and warnings to make good use of time and produce, the result will be twisted personalities who, having interiorized the demands made upon them, can no longer enjoy life. Jacques Philippe speaks with regret of "the narrow-mindedness of those who measure everything according to strict rules . . . [such as:] 'Do not handle, Do not taste, Do not touch,'[17] and make life impossible for others by their merciless legalism or perfectionism."[18]

It is true that Christ asks his disciples to bear fruit,[19] but this exhortation must be understood in the context of the Gospel, not by the standards of productivity. *Fruitfulness* is different from *productivity*. A person can produce much, get results and many rewards for his work, and yet not be really fruitful. Someone else might be unproductive as the world sees it yet be extremely fruitful. Perfection doesn't come from ever-increasing rigor but from living steadily in the light of truth.

Christ asks for fruits that endure.[20] We can be sure that what lasts forever won't be our money or our fame. All that will matter at the end of life will be the love we've offered and received. We shall have nothing else then.

---

17. Col 2:21.
18. Jacques Philippe, *Interior Freedom*, cit., p. 116.
19. See Lk 13:6–9.
20. See Jn 15:8.

But there's a problem: the fruit Christ asks for can't be counted nor measured; it can't be put on display. It is hidden from our sight, and only God, "who sees in secret," knows it.[21] Moreover, God himself is its principal author, since it is produced and grows precisely insofar as someone is united to him.

Guiding Others Toward Great Ideals

Constant criticism of the world we live in accomplishes very little. Someone who is forever lecturing others and predicting doom is hardly attractive. It's far better to teach young people to open and broaden their souls—to direct their yearnings toward great ideals. As matters stand today, the educational process sometimes seems marked by a certain resignation—and not much enthusiasm. Yet even today many young people are restless—healthy rebels against the tendency toward lazy conformity to current fashions. On German television a few years ago, a seventeen-year-old said, "In this society all that counts is money and having a big car. This can't be the meaning of life. For us, what counts are friendship and fellowship." How tragic that this boy was a Neo-Nazi who'd been arrested by the police.[22]

Many people are fundamentally bored by a bourgeois life filled with dead hours spent watching television in their pajamas, with a beer close at hand. The more entertainment they soak up, the more bored they become. So they seek out increasingly absurd things to gratify themselves—just as Nero is said to have burned down half of Rome to amuse himself. What we need to learn instead is responsiveness to

---

21. Mt 6:4, 18.
22. See Fritz Reheis, *Die Kreativität der Langsamkeit: Neuer Wohlstand durch Entschleunigung* (Darmstadt, 1996), p. 123.

nature, to music, to literature, to conversation and friendship, and to commitment to others—including those who see things differently from us. There is an immense panorama for focusing restlessness, awakening interests, and sowing curiosity.

We can help young people discover human dignity and the authentic meaning of life. A young person with lofty goals will struggle zealously to attain them. He is prepared to renounce secondary, trivial things and will see for himself that one must say no. By experience he may learn that work, serving others, friendship, and generosity contribute more to happiness than dressing according to the latest fashions. In this way egoistic consumerism will cease to be a problem, without much needing to be said about it.

Disinterested magnanimity is typical of a good educator. He or she helps young people to find their original path toward God. An educator like this doesn't solve all the student's problems but teaches them how to act freely, by the light of their own reason, without needing to be watched and controlled. In this way educators gradually make themselves unnecessary, step back, and become less and less visible. "They give light because they do not appear, they shine because no one applauds them," as the Orientals say. Yet they enjoy the profound satisfaction of knowing that their students, along with the clear sense of being protagonists of their own lives, have high goals and are eager to reach them.

✑ Epilogue

THE GERMAN POET AND DRAMATIST Schiller says: "Man was created free and is a free being, even if he was born in a dungeon." This truth, so necessary to understand our anxieties and aspirations, is an essential aspect of the Christian message. We are called to live up to our nature with full freedom.[1]

We have been placed for a short time in this world to say—through joys, pains, and sorrows—a great *yes* to the invitation to love extended to us by God. Nourished and strengthened by grace, a Christian can experience a profound interior liberation. He experiences the internal unity that causes something like an explosion of vitality. Thus, he comes to enjoy life and to foster an atmosphere of joy around him.[2] At the end of his life, Pope Paul VI said: "I think that departure should express itself in a great and simple act of acknowledgment and even of thanksgiving. Despite its labor, its shadowy mysteries, its sufferings, its fatal decrepitude, this mortal life is a very beautiful reality, an always original and moving prodigy, an event worthy of being celebrated in joy and in glory: life! The life of man!"[3]

God does not want us to remain in our own narrow world, where we control and calculate everything. He calls us to launch out and fly like eagles, higher and higher, toward the sun, which is Christ.

---

1. See Gal 5:13.
2. See 2 Cor 1:24.
3. Paul VI, *Pensamiento sobre la muerte* (Brescia, 1988).